REFLECTIONS ON A SPIRITUAL JOURNEY

St Vladimir's Seminary Press

Orthodox Christan Profiles Series

Number 1

The Orthodox Christian Profiles Series acquaints the reader on an intimate level with Orthodox figures that have shaped the direction of the Orthodox Church in areas of mission, ascetical and liturgical theology, scholarly and pastoral endeavors, and various other professional disciplines. The people featured in the series are mostly our contemporaries and most remain active in shaping the life of the Church today. A few will have fallen asleep in the Lord, but their influence remains strong and worthy of historical record. The mission of this series is to introduce inspirational Orthodox Christian leaders in various ministries and callings that build up the Body of Christ.

Chad Hatfield
Series Editor

Reflections on a Spiritual Journey

Metropolitan JONAH
(Paffhausen)

Archbishop of Washington
Metroplitan of All America and Canada

Edited by
Virginia Nieuwsma

ST VLADIMIR'S SEMINARY PRESS
YONKERS, NEW YORK
2011

ॐ ॐ ॐ

Publication of this book was made possible by a generous gift from
Dr. Egerton and Anne van den Berg.

ॐ ॐ ॐ

Library of Congress Cataloging-in-Publication Data

Paffhausen, Jonah.
  Reflections on a spiritual journey / Jonah Paffhausen ; edited by Virginia Nieuwsma.
    p. cm. — (Orthodox Christian profiles series ; no. 1)
  ISBN 978-0-88141-880-4
  1. Paffhausen, Jonah. 2. Orthodox Church in America—Bishops—Biography.
3. Orthodox Church in America. I. Nieuwsma, Virginia. II. Title.

BX738.O779P34 2011
281.9092—dc22
[B]
                                                        2011015878

With gratitude to
assistant editor Steve Robinson
and transcriber Jan Bear

ST VLADIMIR'S SEMINARY PRESS
575 Scarsdale Rd, Yonkers, NY 10707
1-800-204-2665
www.svspress.com

ISBN 978-0-88141-880-4

PRINTED IN THE UNITED STATES OF AMERICA

CONTENTS

Foreword

My personal connection to Metropolitan Jonah (in the world—James Paffhausen) dates back to the days after his graduation from St Vladimir Seminary. We were from the same state, California. I graduated in 1982. Jim Paffhausen was a year or so behind me. I went off to be a choir director, and he stayed longer to complete a Masters in Theology. Upon graduation, young Paffhausen worked briefly as a youth worker in Colorado. Eventually he received a blessing to travel to Russia and spent several years at the Valaam Monastery. It was there he developed an important spiritual bond with the abbot of that community and a love for the monastic life. When he returned to California and was ordained to the priesthood, he was sent to care for a series of small mission parishes. He was very involved in the planting and development of missions in the American West (and was shepherding missions up until his last days before his election as Metropolitan). At the same time, the young priest-monk felt called to establish a monastic brotherhood. He was given a blessing to start a monastery at Point Reyes, California. His was not the first to attempt to build a monastic community at the St Eugene Hermitage there. A small group of nuns had become unable to live in that place and had moved elsewhere. Now he would try.

I was aware to one degree or another of Hieromonk Jonah's efforts through the phone calls and correspondence that arrived in the diocesan office where I served as secretary to the bishop. There seemed to be many trials and tribulations. Novices came and went. There did not seem to be much encouragement from the bishop or his chancellor, but Fr Jonah kept at it. There were not many American monastic models to follow that promised success. Orthodox monasticism on our continent up to that time was, with few exceptions, typically the story of a father "superior" and his father "inferior" setting out to found "their own" monastery after having failed to get along in one or another community established by some other father "superior." Father Jonah was determined to break that mold.

With determination, God's blessing and sometimes in spite of outside pressures, the monastery grew. Over the years I was able to visit the Monastery of St John in my capacity as the diocesan archdeacon. We served together on feast days with Bishop TIKHON and the local clergy. There was enthusiastic support from Mr. Constantine Chekene who brought bus loads of people from the Russian community of San Francisco up to Marin County for services. Pilgrims from all over came to the monastery for spiritual guidance and I observed God's blessing in the steady growth of the brotherhood. Several years later, when I returned to the Diocese of the West as an auxiliary bishop, I personally found comfort and support in Fr Jonah and the brothers. I believe monasteries in their best moments are not only places of repentance, but wellsprings of healing in this troubled world.

Eventually due to this steady spiritual and numeric growth, it became clear the original site of the monastery was not suitable any longer. The St Eugene Hermitage in Marin County, just north of San Francisco, had a beautiful chapel, but the other buildings were old, small, damp and had a serious mold problem. The neighbors were not really thrilled about having a big monastery with its accompanying traffic in their midst. Fr Jonah set out to find another location where the community could grow.

It seemed as though he would never find the right place. We spoke several times about his frustrations and I told him God would find the place for His monks, all he had to do was look. Property was found outside of Redding, California, and, with lots of prayer, the brothers took a leap of faith and purchased a forested piece of land with a couple of buildings that seemed to promise room to grow.

More men came to the monastery. The community was becoming the largest men's monastic community in our Orthodox Church in America. Abbot Jonah was constantly on the road raising funds and inspiring the faithful to come and visit St John's through his speaking engagements. There was $500k to raise and the little chapel that was at Point Reyes had to be moved to the new site. There were young novices and a community to forge together. The monastery had publications to get out. Besides all that, there was a constant stream of men and women coming to the monastery for spiritual guidance and respite. So much depended on the person of Abbot Jonah!

In the midst of all this, Archbishop Dmitri of Dallas and the South asked the Holy Synod for an auxiliary bishop to help him administer his rather large diocese because of his age and being close to retirement. Several candidates were interviewed, but the archbishop's attention was drawn to Abbot Jonah of the St John of Shanghai and San Francisco Monastery. The monastery was a real spiritual treasure in my own diocese. I thought, "How in the world could I possibly let this happen?" The monastery had become known for its publishing. Things were just starting to grow. The monks needed their abbot. Who would take over this tiny little but growing flock? New property had been found and a big move made. How would the mortgage be paid off? Would the community begin to decline with the loss of its abbot? But, after some prayer, I came to realize God was indeed calling Fr Jonah to something greater and He would provide for the monks.

And so, I told the Archbishop, the best recommendation I could give him was my great reluctance to let Abbot Jonah go. With some real fears for the monastery's future, I agreed to let Abbot Jonah go to the Diocese of the South to be considered as the auxiliary bishop and chancellor of that diocese. God always provides, and God did provide another wonderful shepherd to care for the monks of St John in Fr Meletios Webber.

Abbot Jonah was elected by the Holy Synod and consecrated Bishop of Fort Worth on November 1, 2008 in the newly frescoed St Seraphim Cathedral in Dallas, Texas.

Eleven days later, all the hierarchs, clergy and lay delegates from across North America gathered in Pittsburgh, PA for our 15th All American Council. We came together at what was a very critical moment in the life of our young Archdiocese. The long-time Chancellor of the Archdiocese had been removed and defrocked. Financial irregularities had been exposed by a Special Investigating Committee.

Metropolitan Herman had retired. The Bishop of Alaska had been retired after an investigation into serious problems in that diocese. The internet was abuzz with all sorts of opinions and rumors. None of the bishops were very anxious to take up the helm. There was a real fear that things were just going to fall apart. In spite of all that, a Metropolitan had to be elected.

The meetings were held in a fairly large room of a local hotel. The bishops were sitting on a dais. At the very far end sat the newly-elected auxiliary bishop from the South. I was rather ill with the flu at the time. I had to leave the meeting from time to time in order to rest. The meeting dragged on. It was late. I got a call: "You had better get down here. Things are not going well." I sighed and got dressed. When I arrived, The Bishop of Fort Worth, the youngest of the bishops of the youngest Orthodox Church in the world had just finished speaking to a rather difficult crowd. The mood had somehow changed. It was as though a window had opened in the room and fresh air had been let in.

The rest, I believe, is history. The very next morning the newly ordained Bishop of Fort Worth was elected the Primate of the Orthodox Church in America. A miracle had somehow quietly taken place. The last had indeed become the first. The abbot of that struggling monastery was elected by the hierarchs, clergy and faithful who had gathered in Pittsburgh to be the Archbishop of Washington and New York, Metropolitan of All America and Canada. His Beatitude's words inspired the Council on that October night and this book presents a few of his thoughts and writings. May they be a blessing to the reader.

+Benjamin
Bishop of San Francisco and the West
Kodiak, Alaska, June 1, 2009

Introduction

"Thou shalt honour him that speaks to thee the word of God, and be mindful of him day and night; and thou shalt reverence him, not as the author of thy birth, but as one that is made the occasion of thy well-being. For where the doctrine concerning God is, there God is present." (Apostolic Constitutions, Book 7: 9)

"In order to write the truth in a godly way, one has to have a mind that sees God."
(Archimandrite John Krestiankin of the Pskov-Caves Monastery)

My relationship with Metropolitan Jonah is complicated. I have known him for a very long time. We met when he was still a college student at the University of California Santa Cruz. I was a very new priest "not yet smelling of incense" as the Russians say. "Jim", as we knew him then, was a young man full of love for our Lord Jesus Christ and zeal for his newly-found Orthodox faith. That love and zeal expressed itself in an insatiable appetite to learn. He wanted to drink deeply from the "wells of salvation," and in so doing, he manifested a joy that was utterly infectious to those around him (cf Isaiah 12:3). As he was working on his own salvation, others around him were being saved. In his learning he was already teaching.

Jim's desire to extract the sweet nectar of piety was not limited to any particular flower. He wanted to hear scholarly theologians and he wanted to hear monastics. He asked questions of parish priests as well as parish grandmothers. He was never much for jurisdictional or ethnic rivalries. As an American convert, it was easy for him to recognize that Orthodoxy existed in all but was exclusive to none. In this spirit he helped organize a multi-jurisdictional Orthodox Christian Fellowship at UCSC, and was instrumental in arranging for speakers to come and give lectures on the campus. One such lecture was given by the late and venerable Hieromonk Seraphim (Rose) from the St Herman of Alaska Monastery in Platina, California (Russian Orthodox Church Outside of Russia). Another was delivered by a relatively new priest from Saratoga, California (Orthodox Church in America).

Besides seeking out those who could help him grow and thrive in the Orthodox faith, Jim also loved to read. I can never remember a time, when he was a student, when he was my choir director, when he served as deacon in my parish, when he was in Russia, etc., when he didn't have a book . . . no, several books, going at the same time. Here too, his choices were varied and eclectic. Books on theology, patristics, history, philosophy, psychology, art, and many other areas, were great sources of consolation and education for him.

All of these things, combined with an excellent seminary education, traditional monastic formation, and loving and supportive parents, made it possible for Metropolitan Jonah to embrace and exercise the gifts of preaching, teaching, and writing which were given to him. That God suddenly chose him to be Archbishop of Washington and New York, Metropolitan of All America and Canada made sense.

Now I would be remiss if I didn't mention one more thing. Another of Metropolitan Jonah's special gifts in the past, as well as today, is that he never imagines any personal interaction to be coincidental or inconsequential. He has always viewed his intercourse with others as having been arranged by Providence as an opportunity for friendship. Christ said "You are my friends" and "I have called you friends" (John 15: 14–15). Metropolitan Jonah is a true image of this virtue. And perhaps that's why I suggested at the beginning, that my relationship with him is complicated. As First Hierarch of our Orthodox Church in America, I understand his role and mine have changed and evolved over the years. But for my family and me, one thing will never change, our friendship.

+Archpriest Basil Rhodes
St Nicholas Orthodox Church, Saratoga, CA

Biography

James Paffhausen, the future Metropolitan Jonah, was born in
1959 to Jim and Louise Paffhausen. It was the tail end of the baby
boom, the era of the birth of rock and roll, Dwight Eisenhower
was president, Mayor Richard Daley ruled Chicago, and the
Paffhausens lived on the North Side, near Lake Michigan.

James' ancestors were German Lutherans and Catholics. The German Lutherans on his mother's side had split into Missouri and Wisconsin Synods, alienating her family from the church. Her father, a wealthy Chicago developer, had lost everything in the Great Depression only to rise to new successes from its ashes, including a major role in the development of Palm Springs, California. James' father's forebears were a long Bavarian priestly line that had provided many clergy and nuns to the Roman Catholic Church in Germany and in America. While James' parents treated the Church with respect and held to a personal faith, they didn't subscribe to any denomination or attend church often. In order to marry Louise, Jim was baptized into the Episcopal Church, and so it was through the Episcopal door that their son James would first discover Christ.

In 1967 eight year old James, three year old Laura, and their parents left the Windy City for California's San Fernando Valley, where in one of life's delicious ironies, the future Metropolitan's father started a mortgage company for Metropolitan Life. By James' tenth birthday the Paffhausens had migrated to La Jolla, a quaint coastal town north of San Diego. As James moved into his teen years, his parents encouraged him to get involved in the youth group at the local Episcopal Church. James was confirmed there, sang in the choir and served at the altar, eventually becoming chief acolyte.

Call and Conversion

When James was 15 he had a life-changing experience. Sitting in his sophomore math class, he was suddenly taken up into the Presence of God, Who spoke to him, not so much audibly, as to his heart: "You are going to be a priest." James wasn't even a committed believer yet and had decided on a career as an architect. He confided this "Damascus Road" experience to his youth minister, who began tutoring him in the Bible. His pastor also encouraged him to read the Church Fathers: first St Irenaeus, and then many others, from the early Church through the Spanish Mystics. James also began attending retreats at the Catholic Benedictine monastery in Oceanside.

Eventually young James read himself out of the Episcopal Church, and began attending Catholic Mass, simultaneously exploring the charismatic movement. By the time he entered the University of California, San Diego, he had thoughts of becoming a priest, but as a blooming Catholic he'd hit an obstacle: he was in a committed, marriage-bound relationship with a young woman from the Episcopal youth group.

On a day that forever changed the course of his life, James wandered into a hippy bookstore in La Jolla and discovered Orthodoxy when he picked up Vladimir Lossky's *Mystical Theology of the Eastern Church*. "After I read the first paragraph, I knew I had no choice but to become Orthodox." He knew no Orthodox Christians and had never attended an Orthodox liturgy, so James went searching for a parish. It was 1977 in San Diego, and he couldn't find any parish using English in the services. After several encounters with priests and parishes that might have made a less determined seeker give up, James found Our Lady of Kazan church (Moscow Patriarchate), the only English speaking parish in one of the largest cities in California, where its Mexican priest, Fr Ramon Merlos, warmly welcomed him, providing a safe incubation with sound catechism. James was chrismated into the Orthodox Church by Fr Ramon on October 12, 1978.

Education and Vocation

Newly chrismated, James transferred to UC Santa Cruz, continuing his studies in Anthropology, Religious Studies, Russian and Greek. Here he helped start an active chapter of Orthodox Christian Fellowship whose members flourished in the faith, later to become four hieromonks (one now a bishop), two abbots, a married priest and his matushka, a deacon, a couple of nuns, and many faithful laymen.

In the Fall of 1979 Bishop Mark (Shavikin) of the Moscow Patriarchate tonsured James a reader. As the last surviving monk of Old Valaam, a monastery in northern Russia, Bishop Mark was a treasury of its stories and rich spirituality, and he planted in James an interest in Valaam that would bear fruit years later. Discipling and guiding James in this critical time of his formation, Bishop Mark tutored him in both the Liturgy and chant in Slavonic.

James discovered St Nicholas, the OCA parish in Saratoga, which, half an hour over the mountains from Santa Cruz, was the closest Orthodox Church. Fr George Benigsen welcomed him and James attended when he couldn't drive two hours north to San Francisco.

Travelling together to Calistoga, California in 1981 James and his godson (who later became Abbot Gerasim of St Herman Monastery in Platina) spent the summer as monastic novices. They especially enjoyed meeting and learning at the feet of Elder Archimandrite Dimitry (Egoroff) and Mother Victoria, Abbess of Our Lady of Kazan Skete in Santa Rosa. The young men provided muscle for the more physical chores and the monastics taught them how to read and sing the services, modeling healthy monastic life. They also met and developed a relationship with Fr Seraphim Rose and with Fr Herman at the Platina monastery two hours north of Calistoga.

James graduated with honors from the Stevenson College of UC Santa Cruz in 1981 with a BA in Anthropology. At the graduation reception a professor pulled him aside and said, "We have been watching you! Of all the crazy things our students get into, this is the wildest: Russian Orthodoxy!" The college also honored James for his work in founding and building up the Orthodox Fellowship on campus. James' great love for the OCF never faltered, and would flower into even stronger and more active support and encouragement in his years as abbot, bishop and then as metropolitan.

With the support of Fr Jonathan Mayo at St Nicholas in Saratoga, and the blessing of OCA Bishop Basil Rodzianko of San Francisco, James looked forward to attending St Vladimir's Seminary in the fall. Still committed to the girlfriend he'd had since high school, monasticism was not in his plan.

Seminary and Graduate Work

James entered seminary in the Fall of 1981 still green in the Faith and confused by some elements of his initial formation as an Orthodox Christian: zealotry, hatred of Roman Catholicism, and what he would later describe as superficial Orthodoxy. Father Alexander Schmemann helped begin to straighten him out, providing him with a more solid footing.

In this time of maturation and growth, James took a year off from seminary to help his father with his mortgage business and earn the money he needed to finish seminary. Realizing that he had to be faithful to his vocation and to the Gospel, no matter how broken the people that populated the Church, he returned to St Vladimir's in September of 1983. Interested in dogmatics and patristics, James focused on Christology, mysteriology and ecclesiology, writing his MDiv thesis on the Eucharistic Theology of the Iconoclast Controversy.

In James' second year at seminary he met Bishop Kallistos (Samaras) of the Greek Archdiocese who taught him the use of the Jesus Prayer and an understanding of the stages of purification and hesychast practice. James spent hours visiting the Bishop's monastery in nearby Astoria, New York, and gained a great appreciation for traditional Greek village style piety. For his parish assignment James served at Holy Trinity Greek Orthodox Archdiocesan Cathedral with Fr Robert Stephanopoulos. Providentially, James was building strong relationships with the clergy of the Greek Archdiocese and developed a love for Greek liturgics he retains to this day.

At seminary James was influenced by the teachings of Fr John Meyendorff and enjoyed times spent with Fr Thomas Hopko, both in class and with his family. James graduated from St Vladimir's with honors in 1985 at the age of 25. Aiming towards a career as a university or seminary professor, but still contemplating the priesthood, James wanted to immediately pursue a PhD, but needing money first, he returned to San Diego to work in the mortgage business. In 1986, James returned to St Vladimir's to work towards a MTh in Dogmatics under the guidance of Fr Thomas Hopko.

During his first year of MTh studies James served as choir director for St Mary Magdalene Mission in upper Manhattan and also sang in the St Vladimir Seminary Octet. Over the summer the Octet visited 100 parishes, expanding the future Metropolitan's vision and experience of the Church in America. He made mental notes on what was working, what was not, what needed some attention, and what needed radical change. James served as spokesman and fundraiser for the Octet.

In the Fall of 1987 James finished his comprehensives for the MTh and began his thesis, "An Orthodox Review of the Ministry Section of the Baptism, Eucharist, Ministry," under Fr Thomas Hopko. To research his subject more thoroughly, he went to Holy Cross Greek Orthodox School of Theology in Boston as an exchange student. He enjoyed the opportunity to once again establish friendships with Greek brethren including (now) Archbishop Demetrios while solidifying his sense that he belonged in the OCA. In May, 1988, James received the MTh in Dogmatics from St Vladimir's.

Towards the end of his MTh work, James served as cantor during Holy Week and Pascha with Fr Timothy Lowe in Colorado and accepted Fr Timothy's invitation to return to Colorado to serve with him as Deanery Lay Assistant. In Colorado, he taught catechism, music and the Late Vocations program and quickly caught the mission-building and teaching bug. Although this ministry was cut short by his need to return to California to help his ill father, James' time in Colorado nourished a compunction in him that would ultimately bear fruit in the many mission parishes he would later plant.

Back in San Diego, James continued to work for the Church while also managing the family commercial mortgage company as his father recuperated from surgery. Serving as parish council president, helping in a building program, editing the diocesan newspaper, running an outreach to Episcopalian clergy with Fr Paul O'Callaghan, and teaching deacons in the Late Vocations Program, James learned the role of active layperson, another foundational experience for him. Eventually, having recovered from his illness, and seeing that James' heart wasn't in the mortgage business, Jim Paffhausen encouraged James to pursue what he knew his son loved best, serving the Church.

In the Summer of 1991, James returned to the Bay Area to pursue his PhD studies at the Graduate Theological Union (UC Berkeley). James remembers this as another major turning point in his life: when he committed himself completely to serving the Church. Fr Basil Rhodes, parish priest at St Nicholas in Saratoga, appointed him choir director and mentored him. Under Archpriest Basil, James gained a sense of the scope of parish ministry, as well as diocesan responsibilities.

At Berkeley James initially elected Spirituality as his PhD concentration but before long switched to Church History. He found the Graduate Union's liberal ecumenical environment a stark contrast to St Vladimir Seminary and came to appreciate more deeply what he later called "the quality of intellectual formation at St Vladimir's, far above many other seminaries across the broad ecumenical spectrum." Many of the students were in their late 40's and, feeling he needed more maturity to fully appreciate the program, 32-year old James left Berkeley after three semesters with plans to come back and finish. With this phase of study behind him, he entered the arena of active ministry.

Russia and Valaam

While still studying for his PhD at the Graduate Union, James had worked as a bookkeeper at Raphael House in San Francisco, then owned and operated by the Christ the Saviour Brotherhood (CSB), formerly the Holy Order of MANS, a well known West Coast New

Age esoteric and philanthropic organization. As the first non-brother-hood employee, he was uniquely positioned to observe the group's difficult but eventually successful struggle to find its way into the Orthodox Church. During this time James heard of and developed an interest in the Valaam Society and the Russkiy Palomnik ("Russian Pilgrim") Mission.

With the blessing of Bishop Tikhon of San Francisco and Los Angeles, James traveled to Moscow to work at the Mission. In Moscow, he struggled at first, since it had been twelve years since he'd studied Russian in college, but tasked with shopping and cooking for the mission, he learned quickly. In the markets of Moscow—and in the churches—he sharpened his linguistic skills as he grew in love for the Russian people.

In the Mission's Publishing Department located at the Patriarchate's offices in Moscow, James was drawn to local monastic communities. In his free time he visited the many churches and monasteries in, around and outside Moscow. Journeying to Valaam, he met Archimandrite Pankratiy, its Abbot, and had many long discussions with him. The two sparked a plan to create a missionary center at Valaam and to re-evangelize Karelia and its surrounds, using American missionaries in cooperation with the Monastery.

Traveling together on a midnight train to Moscow to receive a blessing from the venerable Elder Kyrill, both James and Abbot Pankratiy were reading *St Silouan of Mt Athos*, by Archimandrite Sophrony. They spoke fervently together about St Silouan's vision of mission, and discovered that they had the same heart. Although Fr Pankratiy was only four years older, James saw in this Father what he longed to become. From that moment, Fr Pankratiy became his spiritual father.

Arriving in Moscow after the night train ride, James and Fr Pankratiy met Elder Kyrill in his cell at the Trinity-St Sergius Lavra. Encouraging the two who had come to him for counsel, the Elder blessed the idea of a missionary center. James then asked the Elder a life-changing question: "What should I do? I have a girlfriend in San Francisco waiting for me but I am prepared to serve the Church all my life." The Elder replied, "I know, I know." "What is the will of God for me?" urged James. Elder Kyrill said, "Be a priest monk!" and he blessed him. James knew from the depths of his being that the Elder was right.

In June, when he had completed his commitment at the Russkiy Palomnik Mission he returned to Valaam where the brothers, unsure of what to make of this new American novice, received him cautiously. Eventually their hesitation gave way to warmth and acceptance. During one of the long Valaam vigils, the great Elder Raphael, who had been a monastic for thirty-five years, heard James' life confession. James read a long list of sins and told the Elder about himself. After about twenty minutes, when James paused, the Elder said, "I think you forgot a few things . . ." and he proceeded to tell James about James. "It was the most healing thing that ever happened to me, a profound experience of grace," remembers Metropolitan Jonah.

James returned to Moscow to oversee the Podvorye (the OCA's representation church), planning to go back to Valaam for his tonsure and ordination. Realizing that being tonsured as a monk by the Patriarch would require that James become a Russian citizen and create a confusing mix of obediences, the Orthodox Church in America's representative intervened, asking him to hold off his tonsure until he returned to America . While disappointed, James understood and continued his assigned work for Valaam, communicating with foreign donors and guests and trying to find international financing for the redevelopment of the Moscow Podvorye. During this time he travelled extensively around Moscow and St Petersburg, and back and forth to the Valaam islands.

In early autumn of 1993 the threat of civil war hovered over Russia. With the Parliament building burning and snipers in the streets of Moscow, rumors raged throughout the country and on Valaam the monks, fearing for the safety of their foreign novice, sent James to Susanina, a village east of Petersburg, to Eldress Lyubichka. Revered by the hierarchs and monastics as a pillar of prayer upholding the world, Elder Raphael trusted the Eldress to guide James. Arriving at her home, James asked the Eldress her perspective of the turmoil. Her anguished response was, "Blood, blood! Everywhere, blood!" James then asked, "What about America?" She said, "There too, but not yet."

"What should I do?" James queried. "Go back to America," she replied. "It is safer there for the time being. Help from there." In Russian monastic fashion, that settled the question: James would leave Russia.

Years later, Metropolitan Jonah reflected, "The experience in Russia completely changed my perspective on life and ministry. On one hand, I saw a vision of the life of the Church, and of monasticism in Russia which was focused on the future, though with an awareness of the rich heritage of the past. The Russian clergy, especially the monastics, were deeply and creatively engaged in the current situation, and totally committed to the spread of the Church and the Gospel without compromise. My sense of purpose for my seminary education took on a whole new meaning when I looked at it from this Russian perspective; it now made much more sense to me. I am profoundly grateful for that education and for the experience in Russia!"

Back in America, Fr Jack Sparks of the Antiochian Evangelical Orthodox Mission had been asking James to find two ranking Russian clergy to come to Pasadena, California to address a symposium jointly sponsored by evangelical Fuller Seminary and the Crystal Cathedral, a Los Angeles mega-church. James escorted Fr Pankratiy and Archpriest Dimitri Smirnov from Russia to the symposium where hundreds of conference attendees were meeting to discuss how to spread the Gospel in Russia. James served as a translator for the Russian priests at both the conference and the numerous events and meetings arranged for them. Fr Pankratiy stayed an extra week, visiting the Paffhausen family, St Herman Monastery, and several parishes.

In early December James petitioned for ordination as deacon. On February 6, 1994, at Holy Virgin Mary Cathedral in Los Angeles, Bishop Tikhon ordained James to the diaconate, assigning him to St Nicholas Orthodox Church in Saratoga, California.

Initiating projects near to his heart, James reproduced the music of Valaam with the help of Conciliar Press and planned a pilgrimage to Valaam with Fr Pankratiy for young Americans. Tasked with restoring a building at the Skete of St John the Forerunner, these young adult pilgrims raised money for the materials and traveled to Valaam in two shifts to erect the building. Over fifty people went to Valaam in the summer of 1994, a story recounted by Fr John Oliver in *Touching Heaven*, published by Conciliar Press. The pilgrims were enriched both by living at the Monastery and their time with Elder Raphael. Dn James Paffhausen served as translator. Dn James stayed in Russia for four months, guiding the pilgrims and the building program. During this time at Valaam other heirodeacons trained the newly ordained deacon, a mentoring process he considered invaluable.

The Holy Priesthood

When Dn James returned from Valaam, Bishop Tikhon ordained him to the holy priesthood in Holy Virgin Mary Cathedral in Los Angeles. The newly minted Fr James served close to forty Liturgies in a short span, first in Los Angeles, and then in his formative parish, St Nicholas in Saratoga. Bishop Tikhon then assigned him to establish a mission in the small Northern California town of Merced. Since the fledgling mission could not fully support him, Fr James commuted three hours southeast from his home in Saratoga. His time with Fr Basil Rhodes in Saratoga as a new priest was invaluable, a kind of internship, building on his diaconate training under Fr Basil. For four years he also travelled three hours north once a week to serve the nuns at Our Lady of Kazan Skete in Santa Rosa, a liturgical service that laid broader foundations for his monastic life.

Eventually Fr James moved to Merced to work more closely with the mission parish community. Later he would reflect, "While in Merced I lived alone for about three months. I despise living alone. Eventually I invited some other men to live with me, so we could pray and work the mission together, as a kind of semi-monastic brotherhood. I concluded that community is not optional for me: it is a necessity. While I need solitude, it has its limits."

In June 1995 Bishop Tikhon sent Fr James to St Tikhon's Monastery in Pennsylvania for a time of retreat. When he arrived, the monks told him to prepare to be tonsured to the Small Schema in a couple of days. On the feast of Saint Jonah, Metropolitan of Moscow, June 15, 1995, Metropolitan Herman tonsured Fr James, who became the Monk Jonah. Metropolitan Jonah remains grateful for this pivotal connection to St Tikhon's and his ongoing relationship with the brothers there.

Back in California, since the Merced parish wasn't ready for an active fulltime priest, Fr Jonah received a blessing to establish other missions: first Sonora, located about an hour east of Merced in the Sierras, then Yuba City/Chico, about three hours north, then, establishing contact with a local non-canonical "priest" he began a foundational mission work in Eureka. Interestingly, much of this work followed directly in the footsteps of Hieromonk Alexander Golitzin, who had pioneered mission work in these areas. As the Scripture describes, one plants the seed, one waters, and one reaps the harvest—and today, most of these parishes are thriving and support their own priests. This mission period for Fr Jonah coincided with his serving on the OCA Diocesan Missions Board, and occasionally serving liturgy in Greek for the nuns of St Nicholas Monastery in Dunlap (near Fresno, California). Founded by the Greek Elder Ephraim, the monastery is led by Mother Markella, an Eldress. Fr Jonah enjoyed serving this now full-fledged monastery in its early years of formation.

Monasticism

At the All American Council in 1995, Fr Robert Kondratick asked Fr Jonah to consider taking over the Moscow Podvorye, the Orthodox Church in America's embassy in Russia. Excited about the prospect of returning to Russia, Fr Jonah called Fr Pankratiy at Valaam. Fr Pankratiy asked Fr Jonah, "Why do you want to come over here and be a bureaucrat?" Undeterred, the American priest began taking refresher Russian classes at Berkeley and set his sights on returning to Moscow. After all, he had lived a second life there; he knew the city well, had very strong contacts in the Church and many friends, and he was especially honored as a "baby priest" to have been considered for this important a position. Despite the powerful pull, he waited for his spiritual father, Abbot Pankratiy to give his blessing.

That autumn, Fr Pankratiy visited the United States. As a part of his itinerary, he requested an historic meeting with Elder Ephraim of Philotheou, who was just beginning to plant a series of monasteries in America. Fr Jonah had met the Elder previously, knew some people close to him, and helped arrange a meeting between the two. During that six hour meeting Elder Ephraim laid out his vision for his work in America, explaining his core intent to lay a solid foundation for the Greek community in America—the condition of which concerned the Elder. The Elder Ephraim also gave some direction to Fr Pankratiy as to how internal matters are resolved in Athonite monasteries.

Finally, Fr Pankratiy directed Fr Jonah to submit his question to the Elder: Should he move to Moscow to oversee the OCA Podvorye? The Elder and Fr Pankratiy conferred between themselves then announced to Fr Jonah that his task was not to be a bureaucrat in Moscow, but rather, to establish a monastery in California.

Obeying the Elder, Fr Jonah soon thereafter approached the new chancellor of the OCA's Diocese of San Francisco and the West, Fr Nikolai Soraich, with this directive. Fr Nikolai embraced the idea, and presented it to Bishop Tikhon. Bp Tikhon in turn gave Fr Jonah the obedience to pray the Akathist to St John of Shanghai daily for the establishment of a monastery. Thus began the future monastery's relationship to the San Francisco saint, which continues unabated to this day.

The following spring, a sore in Fr Jonah's mouth began to cause intolerable discomfort and the doctor's diagnosis was cancer. In June of 1996, surgeons removed a third of his tongue and many cancerous lymph nodes. It was an odd illness for someone who had never smoked or chewed tobacco, but the doctors caught the cancer in time, and after six weeks recovery Fr Jonah resumed his ministry. Soon Fr Nikolai contacted Fr Jonah with the news that Bp Tikhon planned to establish a men's monastery in Point Reyes, north of San Francisco, and would be asking Fr Jonah to begin the work there.

One of the men living with him in the Merced brotherhood, Vladimir Phelan, formerly a novice at St Tikhon's Monastery, signed on as the second monk to join the nascent monastery, and on October 31, 1996, Vladimir and Fr Jonah moved from Merced to take over the dilapidated hermitage of St Eugene, in Point Reyes Station, Marin County, California.

St Eugene's Hermitage, built by the Elder Dimitri (Egoroff) in the early 1950's, suffered from neglect and age but it had a beautiful, relatively new chapel. The rest of the grounds and buildings were another story. It took the two monastics weeks to clean up the buildings and make them at least slightly habitable. Built to house only one monk, the hermitage also had a tiny guest house, a classic Athonite style kellion. A few nuns had tried in the past to build a community here, but had grown so ill that they had abandoned the effort of caring for the 17 acres deep in the forest.

Other obstacles soon popped up, evidence of the Enemy's efforts to eradicate the fledgling monastery in this pagan corner of northern California. Hierarchical decisions and lack of financial support severely impacted the work, and made it difficult to survive. Eventually Fr Vladimir decided to move on, and Fr Jonah was alone, despite his profound desire for community. Fr Nikolai gave him the option of sticking it out or moving to Eureka to assume the leadership of a new diocesan parish.

Fr Jonah chose to stick it out. Why? On one of the loneliest days of this period, Fr Dunstan Morrissey, an aged Benedictine Catholic hermit Fr Jonah had never met, wandered onto the Pt. Reyes monastery looking for candles. Quietly speaking with the young monastic about the value of solitude and silence, the relatively ancient Fr Dunstan completely changed Fr Jonah's attitude by the time he left the property. From that time forward, Fr Dunstan remained a strong encouragement, consolation and support to Fr Jonah until his repose shortly after Fr Jonah's consecration as a Bishop.

In June of 1997, God began bringing young men to the monastery at Point Reyes. Young hippies, a Canadian, a young adult from upstate New York, a Southern California native and an older man from Massachusetts all had one thing in common: Each was a new convert. Fr Jonah even baptized the first two who came. The brotherhood exuded young energy and a blissfully ignorant idealism. Fr Jonah didn't feel like he knew what he was doing, but the brotherhood persevered, aided in part by the nuns in Santa Rosa, who shared advice and the cycles of services.

The monastery observed a full daily cycle of services, with Liturgy several times each week. Fr Jonah taught everything since there was no one else who could: the structure of services and how to sing them, along with the basics of monastic discipline. Every weekend he still travelled to missions a couple hundred miles away to support the brotherhood while the brothers attended parishes near Pt Reyes, in San Anselmo or Santa Rosa. Within a year, more brothers had joined, and the monks were running out of space. Within two years, the burgeoning, fluctuating population of ten to twelve novices and postulants all crowded together in the 1,400 square feet of deteriorating buildings.

During this busy period, Father Jonah kept up his former ties, helping some Christ the Savior Brotherhood priests come into the canonical Church and coordinating a fund- raising effort for Valaam. In 1999, the Russian economy collapsed, and Fr Jonah received an urgent call from Fr Pankratiy: Valaam faced either evacuation or starvation, as all their resources had been obliterated when the banks failed. With Bishop Nikolai's blessing Fr Jonah sent out an internet request for emergency help for Valaam. American Orthodox Christians responded generously, and with others' help, Fr Jonah raised over $150,000 for Valaam. This cushion helped Valaam and several other monasteries survive another year.

That winter, Fr Pankratiy invited Fr Jonah to Moscow where the Patriarch could thank him in person. In Russia, the American monk toured many monasteries, seeing firsthand how they'd benefited the American collection. He began to understand why another Elder at Trinity-St Sergius, Nahum, whom Fr Jonah had met early in 1993, had handed him a stack of 10-ruble bills, a prophetic act; and why the Eldress Lyubichka had told Fr Jonah he could help better from America than from Russia.

On his return to San Francisco, Fr Jonah was met by several of his monastery brothers. While Fr Jonah was away, a member of the hierarchy had exploited some tension and personal ambitions in the brotherhood, thus sowing dissension and disturbing the brotherhood. Over the following year, more seeds of discord were planted by those out-side the monastery. A bishop expelled several of the brothers, even though he did not know them personally. Even in the midst of this, God blessed the brotherhood with a visit from Archimandrite Ambrose (Pogodin), who lived with the brothers for a while and was a great sup-port. Looking back on this dark trial, Fr Jonah remembers: "I came very close to simply going back to the world, in grave desperation."

By the end of 2000, Fr Jonah was alone once again at Point Reyes. Like the myrrhbearers, a group of faithful women, his spiritual daugh-ters helped maintain the cycle of services. Thankfully, in the new Mil-lennium a far more stable monastic community was about to form.

The Brotherhood Matures and Takes Root

The dissolution of the first brotherhood was a crushing blow to Fr Jonah, but it didn't take long for new brothers to arrive. The first novice was a young hippy, then a student from Seattle, then others. One man from the first community came back and hung on for a bit, but then left. Within a year there were eight new monks. Though all were new to Orthodoxy (save one monk from Platina, Fr Seraphim Rose's monastery), the character of this new community was more mature, well educated, and stable. Again, Fr Jonah set out to teach everything from the ground up.

Thankfully, the outside hostility died down, but Fr Jonah had learned an important lesson. He was most disturbed that he had not been able to protect the brothers from a hostile outside source that had wreaked havoc in the monastic community, by making pastoral decisions about people without knowing them. Fr Jonah vowed not to let that happen again. Fundamentally rejecting humiliation and abuse as tools to control others, since he believed these to be contrary to Christ and the Church, Fr Jonah determined to do what he could to exorcize the tactics of shame or intimidation from the life of the Church. Others learned from Fr Jonah's brotherhood's struggle. At the next diocesan assembly, a bishop announced to the delegates, "I realize now that the best thing a diocesan bishop can do for a monastery is to leave it alone." Fr Jonah resisted the urge to stand up and cheer.

Life in the community at Pt. Reyes continued apace. One of the brothers who had first arrived was Baruch, a hippy sent to Fr Jonah by the priest in Eureka. Baruch was funny and easy going most of the time, but when he was in a reactive mode he became enraged. This rage came out in various ways, but was usually controlled.

One evening, however, Baruch blew up and stomped out during a meeting with the brothers. After he cooled down, Fr Jonah encouraged him to take a solitary retreat for prayer and reflection, which he did. Afterwards Baruch visited monastery friends on a farm next to the Trinity River, a peaceful setting. But as young men are wont to do, Baruch went rafting on the river in rapids, with no life vest and no helmet. The raft overturned in the rapids, Baruch hit his head on a rock and drowned.

Fr Jonah had gone to Wichita as a retreat speaker, but returned immediately, while the brothers picked up Baruch's body and made funeral arrangements. Over 150 people and ten priests stood for two and a half hours in the rain for the funeral. It was an overwhelming experience of loss, and grace.

Fr Jonah's deep grief over Brother Baruch's death lasted for a long time. Feeling as if he had lost his own son, Fr Jonah later said the incident presented him with the intense experience of what spiritual fatherhood means: to stand with someone at the Throne of God at the Judgement, giving an account for his life and his repentance. He recognized, in his grief, the organic connection between himself and Baruch's salvation.

Baruch's death pulled the brotherhood together with a solid bond. In 2003 brothers began to be tonsured as rasophores, and then to the small schema. This advance transformed the brotherhood into a monastery, with monks now making lifetime vows to the community. The community at Pt Reyes was blossoming despite many distractions.

Fr Jonah longed for a better monastery location. His efforts to redevelop Pt Reyes had been thwarted and he had learned that Marin County building codes would never allow Pt Reyes to grow. Fr Jonah determined to move the brotherhood to a new facility, one that had space for the brotherhood to expand and to host guests, and one that did not have black mold that was causing respiratory problems for nearly all the monks. Fr Jonah, with help from others, scoured the West Coast from Seattle to Monterey, entering into escrow on three properties in Washington State, and then on a piece of land south of the San Francisco Bay area; but all of these attempts ended at insurmountable roadblocks. Finally, the right property appeared, in the beautiful forests near Mt Lassen and Mt Shasta, near the tiny town of Manton.

Fr Jonah took a break from the property search to travel to the Holy Mountain, Athos, in Greece. After stopping in Thessalonica, he went to St Demetrios' Cathedral to venerate the saint. Entering the Cathedral, Fr Jonah saw the saint's relics in their silver sarcophagus in the center of the church, and the saint's Presence filled the entire cathedral. Approaching the relics of St Demetrios, Fr Jonah told him he needed help to get to the Holy Mountain, as his papers had been delayed in the Phanar. Within half an hour, the ladies of the parish swept him up, fed him lunch, and began to talk to him. One said, "Oh, you're having trouble with your papers? My spiritual father is the Protos (head) of the Holy Mountain." She pulled out her cell phone, speed-dialed a number and handed it to Fr Jonah. The Elder spoke perfect English, and all was resolved in a few minutes.

The next morning Fr Jonah went to the Liturgy—it was the Feast of St Demetrios, and the 25 bishops in attendance were serving thousands of people.

After a blessed stay at Vatopedi, Fr Jonah returned to Thessalonica to thank St Demetrios. The Saint's presence overwhelmed him again, but, emboldened, he went up to the relics and thanked Saint Demetrios for the trip. But he had one more favor to ask. "If you can get me half a million dollars to buy a monastery," he vowed, "I'll build a church in your name."

On his return to California, Fr Jonah discovered that the Manton property was available at terms that the monastery could handle. Everything worked together, and the owners carried a note. Thanks to the intercessions of St Demetrios, the monastery was able to raise $500,000 in cash for the down payment; the largest single donation was almost $250,000.

Since moving to Manton in July, 2006, the brotherhood has thrived, quickly outgrowing the 12,000 square foot, 18 bedroom main house. The bedrooms are full, the trapeza is overflowing and the church is packed on weekends. In June 2009 Metropolitan Jonah returned to the monastery to lead the community in consecrating a new chapel. Plans are in the works for additional cells for brothers who continue to come in search of healthy monastic formation.

Journey to the Episcopacy

Starting around 2002 Fr Jonah studied psychology informally, delving deeply into spiritual literature related to the human psyche, trying to understand the interface between modern psychological insight and Orthodox teaching. It seemed as if God was tutoring him, granting him an education by the people He sent who wanted healing from a wide variety of issues: toxic shame, depression, substance abuse, post traumatic stress disorder (PTSD), the effects of child abuse whether physical, emotional, or sexual; and anxiety issues. The Monastery of St John became interested, as a community, in the patristic psychological paradigm for healing.

Fr Jonah also began to study the fathers on prayer, especially St Isaac the Syrian, and to pursue a more focused practice of hesychastic prayer. Encouraged by Fr Dunstan and others, he found this a profound tool for restructuring the soul, and for coming into the experience of God. After moving to Manton, Fr Jonah as Abbot integrated the practice two days each week where the brothers do Matins "on the rope" (that is, praying the Jesus Prayer in their cells, completing a specified number of "laps" on their prayer ropes), and the corporate Jesus Prayer for twenty minutes before each service.

As the brotherhood matured, Fr Jonah developed a number of talks and gave lectures, retreats, and conferences in different parts of the U.S. One set of talks, "Do Not Resent, Do Not React, Keep Inner Stillness," summed up the teaching of Bishop Kallistos, one of his earliest mentors, as well as the teachings of the Philokalia. Fr Jonah also enjoyed speaking at retreats in Canada sponsored by the Ukrainian Orthodox Church in Canada.

As an Abbot, one of Fr Jonah's favorite speaking opportunities was the Orthodox Christian Fellowship College retreat, between Christmas and New Year's. College was pivotal in his life, a time when he began to take his faith more seriously. Fr Jonah encouraged young adults to serve the Church, introducing a summer novice program at the monastery in order to introduce young men to the monastic life in a more intensive, deliberate way.

At Manton, Fr Jonah continued to serve on the archdiocesan Missions Board, and traveled to Redding, CA, and Kona, Hawaii, to help establish new missions. A mission in Susanville, CA, about 100 miles east of Manton, also was built up as a result of the presence of the monks nearby.

At the end of 2007, Fr Jonah was asked whether he would consider being nominated bishop. After all his years of labor, he had just been officially elected and installed as Abbot at St John Monastery. So, as with other decisions, he sent an e-mail message to (now Bishop) +Pankratiy on Valaam, who replied, "What about the monastery? How can you leave the monastery? You don't have a successor." So Fr Jonah put these thoughts on hold.

An old friend, Archimandrite Meletios (Webber), who had retired from parish ministry after 30 years to live in Holland, journeyed to Manton to see whether he could enter the brotherhood as a novice. Fr Jonah knew that Fr Mel was the only one to whom he could entrust the brotherhood, and surprised Fr Mel, when he asked him not only to join the brotherhood, but to consider becoming its new abbot. Fr Mel soon realized that this was the will of God, and as it was also the will of the brotherhood, he accepted the challenge. His "yes" to the brotherhood changed everything, because Abbot Jonah could now entrust his monastery to someone who had both experience and perspective.

During Lent Abbot Jonah went to Dallas to give a retreat, and when he arrived, His Eminence Archbishop Dmitri greeted him very warmly, and after just a few hours, proposed that Abbot Jonah become his auxiliary bishop. The Abbot felt an immediate connection both with Vladyka Dmitri and with the faithful in Dallas. He rejoiced in the spirit of the Cathedral there; it resonated with his vision of what the Church should be as it incarnates the Gospel. Abbot Jonah soon accepted Vladyka's proposal.

In July the Abbot's Bishop, Bishop Benjamin, raised him to the rank of Archimandrite on the Feast Day of St John. Events happened quickly after this: The Synod of Bishops approved his candidacy for Auxiliary Bishop in the South. and at the September Synod meeting, he was elected to the episcopacy. On September 5, he left the Monastery of St John with the novice Gregory, who would become his kellenik (cell attendant) and personal secretary. Before leaving, he tonsured two brothers as rasophore monks. In the ceremony of tonsure, the archimandrite puts the hand of the newly tonsured into the hands of their monastic superior, who will oversee their lives. With this action, emotional and tearful, he handed over the Monastery to Fr Meletios, thus ending a major chapter in his life and ministry.

Bishop-elect Jonah arrived in Dallas, driving a U-Haul and towing a car, on September 11, 2008. Closing escrow on a condo soon after he arrived, he looked forward to settling in. The Diocese and many friends welcomed him warmly, helping furnish his new home. His diocesan administration work began the day he arrived. Soon he was traveling all over this vast Diocese dealing with pastoral issues and problems and serving the Liturgy.

The consecration to the Episcopate was set for Saturday, November 1, the day before Archbishop Dmitri's 85th birthday. The consecration was done by four bishops: Archbishop Dmitri of Dallas, Bishop Tikhon of Philadelphia, Bishop Benjamin of San Francisco, and Bishop Alejo of Mexico City. Spontaneous informal southern hospitality overflowed, with over 400 people who had come to Dallas from around the country feasting on the Texas barbeque in tents, picnic-style. The Archbishop's birthday extended the party, with the revelers enjoying another immense meal and the beautiful fall weather.

Eleven days later, at the All American Council in Pittsburgh, in a move anticipated by no one, the Council elected Bishop Jonah as Metropolitan of the Orthodox Church in America.

By Virginia Nieuwsma

PART I

The Spiritual Life

CHAPTER 1

Forgiveness and Reconciliation

(Published in *The Handmaiden*, Conciliar Press, reprinted with permission)

What is forgiveness?

+Jonah: To forgive means to restore a bond of love and communion when there has been a rupture. Sin ruptures our relationship with God and others, as also do offenses taken and given among people.

When the bond is broken with other people, we tend to objectify them and judge them, not seeing them as persons, but only as objects of our anger and hurt. This is our sinful reaction. We categorize people in terms of their transgression against us. The longer we nurture the anger and alienation, the more deeply the resentment takes hold in our heart, and the more it feeds on our soul. Resentment is a cancer that will destroy us if we don't forgive! It also leaks out and damages our relations with others when we slander and gossip about those who have offended us and try to draw others to our own side. Of course, no one should want to hear such things—but we do!

Forgiveness means overlooking the sin or transgression, and restoring a bond of love. It does not mean justifying the offensive action or accepting it as right, nor does it mean justifying one's own anger or sinful reaction. Forgiveness means laying aside our judgments of the other person and our own sinful reactions, and accepting others for who they are. God's forgiveness of us and our sins against Him is unconditional and absolute. God does not reject us, objectify us, or bear anger or resentment against us. These are, I think, our projections onto God of our own issues and judgments against ourselves when we sin. God does not punish us. Rather, by alienating ourselves from God, we punish ourselves and ascribe this punishment to Him. We turn in on ourselves in anger and self-hatred, and thus shatter our personhood, cutting ourselves off from His love.

By asking God for forgiveness, we open ourselves to His love and acceptance, His grace and compassion. These were there already, but we neglected them. By confessing our sins, we surrender these areas of our lives where we have justified our self-alienation from God. Repentance means not only turning away from sin, but also turning to God. Judas was remorseful for his sin—but hanged himself. We need not only to be remorseful, but also to open ourselves to God.

How are reconciliation and forgiveness related?

+Jonah: Reconciliation presupposes forgiveness. If we forgive someone, we need to be open to reconciliation, if possible. Reconciliation is forgiveness in action—the actual restoration of the interpersonal bond between two people, in mutual acceptance of each other for who each one is.

Forgiveness and reconciliation can lead to a stronger bond than previously existed. Each time an offense occurs, we can learn more about both the other and ourselves. This can lead to a deeper knowledge and understanding of each by the other, and thus can also lead to a more authentic bond of intimacy. Reconciliation should always be the goal.

Sometimes we feel unable to reconcile—to put forgiveness into our actions and restore a relationship. If the person has severely abused us or our trust, it may not be wise to do so. Or perhaps the person is gone or dead. We can still forgive them, pray for them, and accept them—if only at a distance. We need to look at what is in ourselves that prevents us from reconciling—some fear or expectation of the other. But it is crucial to remember that forgiveness is only fulfilled in reconciliation.

An example of God's forgiveness—and a model for our own—is the parable of the Prodigal Son. Think of the hurt of the father as the young son withdrew into the most selfish kind of rejection and rebellion. The father never ceased to love the son, and was watching and waiting for his return. When the son came to himself, and became aware of his own sin—but not of how much he had hurt his father—he returned. Still thinking only of himself and his own needs, he rehearses how he will ask his father to receive him and make him an employee. But his father doesn't even let him finish his little rehearsed speech. He embraces the son and holds him to himself. He has a robe and ring brought, restoring him as son and heir. He kills the fatted calf as a sacrifice of thanksgiving to God. He neither demands nor wants an apology, nor does he permit any justification or even self-denigration on the part of his son. Rather, he forgives his son from the abundance of his love, casting away any resentment or bitterness, and accepts him for who he is—his beloved son.

This is how God forgives us! So we must forgive each other and be reconciled.

Why is it so hard to forgive those closest to us?

+Jonah: The deeper the bonds of love and intimacy, the sharper the pain of alienation through offenses. The more we truly know someone, the more cutting off the bond of love cuts to the core of who we are. We cannot define ourselves solely in an individualistic, autonomous manner. This is a falsehood, our own egocentrism. Who we are, as Christians, as persons, is a mystery hidden in Christ of our union with one another. A husband and wife are one flesh in Christ. "My brother is my life," said St Silouan.

There is a sacred bond of love in friendship, whether in the world or in a monastery. We must be very watchful so as to preserve that bond. But the greater the intimacy is, the greater is the likelihood of deep offenses occurring—because intimacy presupposes vulnerability. This, however, is an aspect of how we grow in knowledge of one another—constant forgiveness and reconciliation. We come to know and accept the other person for who they are. We hopefully begin to recognize our projections and expectations and drop them. Then, we come to know ourselves better through others.

Forgiveness is hard—but it is infinitely sweeter when we reconcile with someone we deeply love. It is hard because it makes us look at our selfishness, our judgment, our expectations, and ourselves. It also shatters the illusions and false objectifications that we have had of the other person, not to mention of the offense itself.

When we have old wounds, even from childhood, we are all the more likely to project onto others our ideas and expectations, which are even more distorted by the old resentments. This is delusion. Our old wounds and resentments may be completely unconscious. They may have been caused by an entirely different person. For example, we project our issues with our parents onto those with whom we develop a close bond. This is the normal dynamic not only of newly married couples, but also of employees with bosses, of students with teachers— and especially, of novices and monks or nuns with their abbot or abbess. When we transfer old unresolved issues onto someone, our idea of that person has very little to do with the person him- or herself. We dredge up old issues with them, and put all the energy of the old resentment into it. This, of course, can destroy relationships.

How do you get out of this? I'm not sure—other than by patience, perseverance, and unconditional love. You have to somehow break through the delusion and see who the person really is.

If we are repeatedly irritated by a person we are close to, it is not their problem, but rather our own. The irritation is our reaction. They are being who they are—and if we have not realized that yet, then we must simply accept them with their character flaws and all. The other person is responsible for his own sins. But I alone am responsible for my reactions.

We have to let go of our resentments of other people, and especially of those closest to us. First, we need to ask ourselves if we want to be angry, bitter, resentful, and unhappy. Then we must look at and take responsibility for our own reactions. We can only change ourselves. Then, we need to try to see the other for who he/she really is, with strengths and weaknesses, sins and foibles, and simply love him/her. This is the basis of forgiveness. Then, we must resolve not to let these things get in the way of that love. We also have to know ourselves. If we admit our own sins and shortcomings, how can we judge anyone else for their sins and failings? It is utter hypocrisy.

Letting go seems hard, but once we do it, we have the most freeing sense of having been liberated from slavery to these demons. First, we need to pray, and ask God to show us ourselves, and to help us to love and forgive. Next, we need to be quiet, and let God show us. He will! Then, we need to be watchful, so that we do not allow ourselves to nurse resentment and bitterness.

What about when I've forgiven, then see the person or hear of him or her, and the old hurt/anger returns afresh? Does this mean I haven't forgiven?

+Jonah: When we still have an angry reaction to someone, it means that we still have some resentment against them. Forgiveness comes in stages. We may be able to forgive partially, but the roots of the resentment are deep in our passions. So, we still have work to do. This is especially true when it is someone close to us, who really matters to our life. An offense can threaten a relationship that is part of our very identity, so the roots of our reactions can be very deep. Our forgiveness is relative to the degree to which we are free from our continued angry or hurt reaction. When we can love and accept someone without remembrance of the wrong, and without a reaction of anger and hurt, then we have truly forgiven.

Another aspect of this is when we are projecting our expectations onto a person, and they continue to disappoint us. This should show us that our expectations are simply our own selfishness, and that we are failing to love the other unconditionally. We must take responsibility for our own anger and hurt, and simply let the person be him/herself.

If the other party refuses to acknowledge an offense or show any remorse for his or her part in the breach, what should I do?

+Jonah: The way of humility is to ask forgiveness, and in turn, at least internally, forgive the offender. It does no good to hold onto offenses and to remember wrongs. Let them know how important the relationship is to you. But then the ball is in their court. You cannot force anyone to forgiveness.

We often work through things verbally—yet we feel guilty when we discuss struggles or anger with another person. Is there a proper place for talking about a problem we're having, with a friend or confidant?

+Jonah: One role of a spiritual father or mother is to be able to help you work through your anger with someone. It is much easier to talk to your friends and acquaintances, but what that leads to is often a disaster: gossip and slander, self- justification and blaming, seeking sympathy, judgment and condemnation. And soon the person whom you resent is excluded from the community. One should never use a group of friends to talk through resentments and bitterness; while they may support your position, they will seldom make you see or take responsibility for your own sin. Guilt in such a case is very healthy, because you have sinned. How seldom it is that we will admit our responsibility for our own reactions among our friends! If we have a close confidant, then perhaps we can talk it through with them. But they need to be impartial, and you must never try to justify yourself or force the other to judge the one who offended you.

How do we cultivate a spirit of forgiveness and reconciliation, so that offenses don't stick?

+Jonah: We can cultivate a spirit of forgiveness by "never allowing the sun to go down on our anger." This is a fundamental monastic and Christian precept. If we allow a resentment to take root, it is our sin, no matter what the other person has done to us. Now, we are only human, and this is part of our fallenness. But, when we see it happening, we need to stop ourselves, recognize that we are no different and sin no less than the other, and forgive. Even to seventy times seven, day in and day out.

When someone says or does something to offend us, intentionally or unintentionally, we do not need to react in any way. We can simply take it in, and respond appropriately. This is the principle of nonreaction. It is based on the realization that our reactions are purely our own responsibility, and not caused by a provocation. The provocations will come, but we can choose to react or not, respond or not.

There is a story in the desert fathers about a young novice who was told by his elder, "Go and yell at the rock." So, for half a day, he went and yelled at a rock, insulted, berated, and cursed it. He went back to his elder, who told him, "Now, praise and flatter the rock." So he went back and praised, flattered, and said nice things to the rock. He went back and his elder asked him, "How did the rock react when you praised it?" "It didn't," he said. "How did it react when you screamed at it and cursed it?" "It didn't react," he said. "So," said the elder, "should you also be impervious to praise or calumny, and react to both in the same way, as did the rock."

Much of the spiritual life is dedicated to one goal: complete self-mastery, especially in relation to control over one's reactions. The more mature we are, spiritually, the greater control we have over our reactions. In other words, we have to be watchful over our thoughts, and maintain a spirit of love and compassion. When our thoughts accuse others, and we begin to be upset, then we need to cut off the thoughts and recognize that they are temptations. They are more about me than about the other person. The more we let our thoughts against the other fester, the harder it will be to rid ourselves of them, and resentments will develop. The basic principle of non-reaction, not only in deed, but in thought and feeling, and maintaining a spirit of peace, is the key. With this underlying attitude, it becomes difficult to get us to take offense, and thus, there is seldom a need for forgiveness or reconciliation. This, however, is a mark of very great maturity, and few there are that possess it.

When I've had a serious disagreement with someone, and we have difficulty speaking comfortably to one another, what should I do?

+Jonah: If we have had a serious disagreement, and cannot speak comfortably with one another, then we need to humble ourselves and ask forgiveness for having offended the other. We have to take responsibility for our part. Then it is up to the other to forgive in return. Always return forgiveness when it is asked.

What are the roots of unforgiveness? What does it do to me if I harbor bitterness? What does it do to the other person? What are the corresponding healing virtues for this passion?

+Jonah: The roots of unforgiveness are pride, vainglory, arrogance, and conceit. If I refuse to forgive someone, it is my sin. I can no longer pray the Lord's Prayer without damning myself, nor approach the Chalice. We refuse to forgive because we feel justified in our resentment and bitterness. We cast all the blame and criticism on the other, and blind ourselves to the reality of our own faults. Thus we live in delusion. To harbor bitterness is unadulterated pride and conceit, and we alienate ourselves from Christ. Resentment and bitterness are cancer in the soul, which will destroy us if we do not forgive and become reconciled. Such bitterness is often the root of addictions, which are simply attempts to anesthetize the pain of our own self-condemnation. We torment ourselves with the remembrance of wrongs and wallow in our self-pity, thinking ourselves the innocent victims. Seldom is this the reality, except in some cases of abuse. When we have rage built up within ourselves, which has been stored up perhaps for years, maybe as the result of abuse or victimization, the process becomes far more complex. It takes a long time to work through such rage, so that our reactions do not come out sideways.

Christ is the ultimate example of complete forgiveness, of non-reaction, and of authentic humility. He did not revile and curse His captors and tormentors, those who slandered Him, bore false witness against Him, even tortured and crucified Him. "As a sheep led to the slaughter, and as a blameless lamb is dumb, so He opened not His mouth." We have countless examples of Christian martyrs bearing all kinds of torments and sufferings for Christ's sake, in a spirit of forgiveness, peace, and reconciliation.

When we truly are innocent victims of someone else's sins, the only thing to do is to forgive them. If we harbor resentment, we repeatedly victimize ourselves with the sin of the other every time we remember their wrong and indulge in our resentment. Forgiveness is the only way to healing.

Sometimes people refuse to receive our forgiveness. To refuse forgiveness is pride and conceit, self-justification. If someone does not want to be forgiven— often because he cannot or will not forgive himself—our forgiveness and compassion is like "burning coals heaped on his head." So also is God's forgiveness of us: not to judge or condemn us, but to lead us to repentance.

The burning coal of love is torment when we refuse to accept forgiveness or forgive ourselves. We cannot accept love when we hate ourselves. But it is precisely this divine love which will heal us because it exposes our self-hatred. In self-hatred we are too ashamed to accept forgiveness, are closed in on ourselves, fearing that exposure of ourselves to ourselves. And so we act out. But if we can turn, repent, and begin to let in the love of God and of others, then that love can begin to transform our souls.

We can only fight against the spirit of pride, unforgiveness and self-condemnation with humility, love, and compassion. Humility does not mean bowing and scraping. Rather, it is being nakedly honest with oneself and others. We have to speak the truth in love; but we can only do this in the brutal honesty of humility, seeing our own sins and realizing the other is no different from ourselves. We can address offenses, but if there is no love in our speech and attitude, there is no truth, only facts. And facts do not heal, only love and compassion.

What does real reconciliation look like? How come we see so few examples of this in action, in the Church, and so many instances of broken fellowship and relationships?

+Jonah: Real reconciliation means complete and authentic acceptance of one another, despite sins, offenses, and transgressions: an authentic bond between persons in a spirit of love and humility. There will always be sins and offenses. We must never allow ourselves to criticize and judge one another, because it is always hypocrisy. We only judge others because we see in them our own faults and insecurities mirrored back to us. But if we can live in mature forgiveness and communion with others, in humility accepting one another as God accepts us, then our communities and churches will be transparent—revealing the Kingdom of Heaven, filled with divine grace.

The sad reality of our churches and lives, marriages and friendships, is that we are fallen, broken, and passionate. We justify ourselves in arrogant conceit, and refuse to forgive or to see our own faults. So our communities shatter, marriages break up, and friendships end. Ultimately, this is because we put the gratification of our egos as the main criterion of relationships, rather than the humble and unconditional love of the other that is demanded by the Gospel.

How often is the lack of forgiveness at the heart of our parish battles, of our marriage problems, and of our problems with our kids?

+Jonah: Lack of forgiveness is the core of almost all our parish battles. Marriage problems and relationships with our kids also have lack of forgiveness at the core. Resentments build up and fester, we heap selfish expectations on one another and can't see one another for who we really are. So it's no wonder that relationships break down. To have a spirit of forgiveness means to be authentically open to one another, despite wrongs and sins. If we can do this, there is nothing that cannot be healed.

CHAPTER 2

Through the Cross, Joy Comes into All the World

REFLECTIONS ON THE MEANING OF SUFFERING

> Jesus said, "The Son of Man must suffer many things, and be rejected by the elders and chief priests and scribes, and be killed, and be raised the third day." Then He said to them all, "If anyone desires to come after Me, let him deny himself, and take up his cross daily, and follow Me" (Luke 9:22f).

The Passion of the Christ

This Lent, multitudes of Americans have flocked to see "The Passion of the Christ," Mel Gibson's graphic depiction of the last hours of the Lord Jesus. This film depicts the sufferings of Jesus in a radical way, nearly impossible to watch in its brutality. It is a kind of an icon in film, though it is one alien to the Orthodox Tradition.

The Orthodox Church's iconography, as well as its liturgical texts, do not dwell on the physical and psychological sufferings of the Christ. Jesus is always depicted dead on the Cross, at peace, in a gesture of complete acceptance of all that happened to Him, and embracing all in the cosmic pronouncement of forgiveness, "Father, forgive them, for they know not what they do." Neither does our theology focus on the physical suffering of Jesus as the ultimate "work of Christ." The Orthodox Tradition focuses on who Jesus is, which is revealed by His work. While we in no way negate the sufferings of Jesus, we see them in the context of the whole economy of salvation, as one aspect of our redemption and salvation. It is the Son of God Incarnate who suffered in the flesh, for us and for our salvation, at our hands. As Orthodox, we can say, as do all other Christians, He suffered and died for me, for my sins, because of my sins. But there is more to it. His suffering and death, and resurrection from the dead, reveal Who He is; but, they also reveal to us who we are, and show us how to endure suffering and transform it.

The churches from the Roman Catholic tradition, Papal, Protestant, Evangelical and Charismatic, focus on the suffering of Jesus as the very act of redemption. This focus of the Western tradition comes from the theological development of their doctrine of the atonement. This rests on profoundly different presuppositions from the Orthodox Tradition.

The Satisfaction Theory of Atonement

The Western tradition is predominantly based on the 11th century writings of Anselm of Canterbury, and his "satisfaction theory of the atonement," then later, for many Protestants, on John Calvin's penal substitution theory from the 16th century. For Anselm, it takes an infinite sacrifice to propitiate the wrath of God, whose honor was infinitely offended by man's sin. Thus, it took the Son of God to become man, to provide that infinite satisfaction, since no other sacrifice could satisfy the wrath of the Father. Anselm, coming from the Orthodox Tradition of the West, was still primarily interested in Who Jesus is. However, the new presupposition introduced by Anselm is that God is infinitely offended, and it is God who must be reconciled to man, and must be propitiated.

For the Orthodox, Christ's death expiates (does away with) the effects of sin that prevent man from knowing God and accepting His forgiveness: Man was alienated from God. For Anselm, it is God who is alienated by man's sin, and who must be propitiated in order to save man, where only the suffering and death of the Son of God can satisfy the debt. For the Orthodox, Christ's sufferings and death show that Christ truly accepted our nature and all its brokenness by His incarnation in order to heal it by the resurrection. We enter into that healing of our nature and relationship with the Father by our own acceptance of the cross. We are purified and illumined through repentance, and made partakers of Christ's resurrected life through grace.

For Anselm, the work of Christ culminates in his self-sacrificial suffering and death, propitiating God the Father by the infinite suffering that He voluntarily accepted to endure as the Incarnate God, and thus reconciling God to man by that infinite satisfaction. A legal transaction is made, and man is saved by accepting that justification by faith, and thereby transferred from the category of the damned to the saved. The Western model is a juridical, forensic idea. For the Orthodox, Christ reconciled humanity to God, and it is our dynamic relationship with God, our obedience in communion with Him, that is our salvation. This obedience is made possible by the gift of the Holy Spirit from Pentecost on, uniting us in Christ and synergizing our life with the grace of God. The Orthodox model is a dynamic idea of communion.

John Calvin and later writers accept the Anselmian tradition as their basic set of presuppositions. Calvin took it a further step, and developed a doctrine of atonement that focused on punishment. Jesus' sufferings constituted an acceptance of God's punishment for the sins of all mankind, as a substitutionary sacrifice and propitiation of God's wrath. Christ vicariously endured the punishment for the sins of all mankind to appease the wrath of God, and thus made satisfaction of the debt humanity owed to God. Thus, Christ suffered the punishment of God's cumulative wrath against man's sin, vicariously suffering in our place, so that we do not have to suffer that punishment.

This doctrine explains the bloody, tortured images of Christ crucified in agony upon the Cross in the Western tradition, whether in painting, statues, or the movie "The Passion of the Christ." Christ's suffering, His agony and death, propitiates the wrathful Father, so that if we believe in it, His suffering substitutes for our punishment and saves us from the wrath of God. This approach makes the resurrection secondary in importance, and in reality, not even necessary (except perhaps as a rational proof that Jesus was qualified to be that sacrifice).

47

An Orthodox Approach to Christ's Suffering and Our Own

As Orthodox Christians, we have an entirely different set of presuppositions about God, about Christ and His suffering and resurrection, and our relationship to them. Christ assumed our suffering, pain and death out of love for us and thus to abolish death and make all things new. By death he overcame the power of sin, and by obedience overcame sin itself. Punishment does not even enter into the Orthodox understanding of redemption; this comes from Calvin. The idea of satisfaction is also alien, coming from Anselm's medieval paradigm of chivalry. In Orthodox thought, God's infinite mercy and compassion is the focus of our vision, not being "saved from the wrath of God" as some translations distort the Bible itself to justify the Protestant presuppostions. A prime example is in Romans 5:9 where the New King James, which fairly reflects the Greek in this verse, reads: "Much more then, having now been justified by His blood, we shall be saved from wrath through Him." In the RSV, it reads, "much more shall we be saved by Him from the wrath of God." In Romans 3:25 the NKJ reads, "whom God set forth as a propitiation by His blood, through faith, to demonstrate His righteousness, because in His forbearance God had passed over the sins that were previously committed . . . " The concept of "propitiation" (which refers to appeasement of the wrath of the Father by blood), instead of "expiation" by blood, (the removal of sin), is a key difference in understanding. The meanings and the objects of the verbs are very different: Propitiation means to appease the wrath of the Father; whereas expiation means to do away with sin. The use of "propitiation" is based on this medieval theological tradition.

The Son of God assumed our humanity in order to bring it to its fulfillment, and thus He had to assume our fallenness that He might heal our brokenness. The healing and fulfillment of our humanity is the Resurrection. He suffered and died to show us how to endure suffering, and to give meaning to our own suffering and death. He accepted the Cross so that we might be able to bear our cross. He fulfilled the Law and was obedient to the Father to the point of death, showing what obedience is. Jesus revealed to us that God is our loving Father who suffers all things for the sake of our salvation.

God the Loving Father

For God so loved the world that He gave His only begotten Son, that whoever believes in Him should not perish but have everlasting life. For God did not send His Son into the world to condemn the world, but that the world through Him might be saved (John 3:16–17).

God the Father sent His Son to reconcile us to Himself out of love for us who had fallen into disobedience and corruption. Jesus came and revealed God to us, and reconciled us to Him as our Father. Jesus revealed not a wrathful God who needs to be propitiated, but the merciful and long-suffering Father who awaits the repentance of his rebellious children. He reveals also that the sinful world constituted by the passions must be overcome, because it is death and the rejection of God. Jesus reveals this "world" as suffering, the passions, the source of which is death, which leads us to sin. Jesus overcomes the world by overcoming sin and death by accepting to suffer. He overcomes sin by obedience, restoring man's communion with the Father in his own humanity in order that we might not lose hope. By that union with the Father He overcomes death and is raised from the dead. He gave His mortal body as a ransom to death and shattered Hades by descending to its depths as God. The death of Jesus was the death of the Incarnate God. His death and resurrection was a cosmic event, radically transforming the nature of creation. His death and resurrection were universal in scope:

> In the tomb with the body,
> in hades with the soul,
> in paradise with the thief
> and on the throne with the Father and the Holy Spirit
> wast Thou O Christ, filling all things! (Orthodox Paschal hymn)

Self-Offering in Obedience

Jesus accepted to suffer and die and to be raised from the dead out of love for us and for our salvation. He came to earth to recapitulate humanity in Himself, to assume it and heal it. Human beings had fallen into sin and corruption. The Son of God came into the world and became a man to raise humanity from corruption and death. He came to save man from the effects of sin and the tyranny of the devil. As God Incarnate He bore in His humanity, not the wrath of God, but the accumulated wrath of human anger and rejection of God by all humanity, all the effects of sin and rebellion, in order to overcome them.

> Let this mind be in you which was also in Christ Jesus, who, being in the form of God, did not consider it robbery to be equal with God, but made Himself of no reputation, taking the form of a bondservant, and coming in the likeness of men. And being found in appearance as a man, He humbled Himself and became obedient to the point of death, even the death of the cross. Therefore God also has highly exalted Him and given Him the name, which is above every name, that at the name of Jesus every knee should bow, of those in heaven, and of those on earth, and of those under the earth, and that every tongue should confess that Jesus Christ is Lord, to the glory of God the Father (Phil 2:5–11).

Jesus bore the cross of obedience to the point of death. He bore the cross of humility, of self-emptying, not holding on to his equality with God the Father. This self-emptying of all the prerogatives of His divinity, all the qualities of His Divine Nature, was necessary because otherwise He could not be human in every way that we are. Jesus became every thing that we are by nature, that He might make us everything that He is by the gift of grace. He reconciled man to God. Man had been alienated from God and persisted in the vanity of rebellion, and had to be reconciled to the unconditionally loving and forgiving God who patiently waited for man's repentance. Because of fear of death (Heb. 2:15), humanity was in bondage to sin—rebellion against God. By destroying death, He destroyed the power of sin (I Cor. 15:56). His obedience overcame that rebellion, and in His humanity He remained in unbroken communion with the Father despite the suffering and despite death. "For as by one man's disobedience many were made sinners, so also by one Man's obedience many will be made righteous" (Rom 5:19).

Jesus suffered at the hands of the leaders of His own chosen people, and was rejected as He had frequently prophesied, that He might reconcile them and all humanity by His own self-offering on the cross. He had to be rejected and had to be killed in order to work salvation and bring about the New Covenant. Jesus is the Law Incarnate, the very God of Abraham, Isaac, Jacob and Moses, and the Creator of the universe. He had to be rejected by those under the Law, the people of the Old Covenant, who themselves recapitulated all humanity, to bring about the New Covenant and to free humanity from the curse of the Law. He accepted to be cursed under the Mosaic Law to show that obedience to God in communion transcends the written Law. He was faithful to the point of death, obedient to the Law, obedient to the will of the Father, that the Law might be fulfilled. He ended His life with the words, "It is finished." With those words, the Mosaic Covenant was brought to a close, and the New Covenant of communion with God by grace was sealed in His blood. From high on the cross He forgave those who tortured and murdered him, not only the soldiers and the Jews, but all humanity. Dying, offering himself to the Father in love for broken humanity, He healed the full brokenness of human nature by rising from the dead and making our human flesh to be a partaker of eternal life.

The Old Covenant was fulfilled by Jesus' obedience; and it was brought to an end by the Jews' rejection of their God as Jeremiah prophesied, that the New Covenant might come into effect. The new covenant is written in the blood of Christ's self-offering in love to the Father. By offering Himself to the Father He expiated the sin of all humanity. Thus the Cross becomes the altar of the New Covenant, the mercy seat and place of expiation of sin, and the very place where the Glory of God dwells, shining forth from the face of Jesus Christ crucified for us.

"Now is the Son of Man glorified, and God is glorified in Him" (Jn. 13:31). Jesus glorifies God by His suffering, by His self-offering in love, by His obedience, by His unbroken love, hope, and faith in the Father, and thus overcomes all suffering. For what is the purpose of the evil one but through suffering to make us lose hope and to break our relationship with the Father? And so God's Glory, the radiance and uncreated energies of His presence, shine forth from the face of Christ the Victor over sin, dead on the Cross.

Jesus' Suffering and Our Own

Jesus did not suffer in order to abolish suffering in this world. He accepted to suffer so that He might accompany us in our suffering, being like us in everything except for sin. He takes on suffering so that He might show us how to hope in the midst of suffering, that it need not lead to despair. Despair, the loss of hope, is in essence the fear of death, and thus the root of sin (Heb. 2:15). He shows us how to accept suffering without despair, by revealing that though we feel abandoned by God in the midst of our suffering, that God has not abandoned us and will raise our life from corruption. God does not abandon us or reject us in our suffering; rather, it is we who abandon Him in despair. Jesus confronted the despair of death, hanging on the Cross, and cried out in the words of the Psalm, "My God, my God, why have you forsaken me?" But the Psalm continues, a song of hope and praise:

> "But You, O LORD, do not be far from Me; O My Strength, hasten to help Me! . . . I will declare Your name to My brethren; in the midst of the assembly I will raise offspring of Israel! . . . For He has not despised nor abhorred the affliction of the afflicted; nor has He hidden His face from Him; but when He cried to Him, He heard him" (Ps 22:19–25).

The temptation of suffering is despair, to lose hope and to abandon God. Christ remained faithful, freely giving Himself over to God at the culmination of his suffering: "Father, into your hands I commit my spirit" (Lk. 23:46).

Death is not the end, as Jesus showed us, indeed gave us, by His resurrection. Our life in this world, dominated by sin and the power of death and the devil, is revealed as simply a passage into the eternal life of the Kingdom of God. The resurrection of Christ was the fulfillment of faithful endurance to the end; so also, our resurrection is the fruit of Christ's sufferings. It is that resurrected life which gives us, as to the martyrs and saints of all ages, the hope that enables us to endure all manner of suffering. It identifies our suffering with that of the Lord Jesus, making it redemptive. As St Paul was able to say, "I now rejoice in my sufferings for you, and fill up in my flesh what is lacking in the afflictions of Christ, for the sake of His body, which is the church" (Col 1:24).

Suffering itself is not sin nor a curse. Rather, it is a moment of judgment, a crisis in the Greek sense of the word. Whatever kind of suffering it may be, if we remain faithful to God, if we hope in Him, we will be able to bear whatever comes. This is what it means to bear our cross: to surrender ourselves completely to God's providence in faith and hope, to love until the end, despising the shame.

Hope and faith are the very means of our relationship with God, the means of our communion and synergy. Suffering endured for Christ, in faith and hope, makes us confront ourselves and cleanses us from all our selfish fears. Thus, suffering itself, endured for Christ's sake, becomes a means of communion with him, purifying us of all that is in rebellion against God. This communion is itself the very essence of joy.

Life in this world inevitably includes suffering. The life of this world passes away, and its suffering has an end. Christ accompanies us in our suffering, giving us hope in the assurance that He has overcome the world by revealing to us the Resurrection. In this is the substance of our hope that enables us to bear all things by the grace of Christ.

The Paschal hymn is very essence of the Gospel:

Christ is risen from the dead, trampling down death by death, and upon those in the tombs bestowing life!

CHAPTER 3

Becoming Our True Selves

(Adapted from an Audio Transcript of a Retreat given in Santa Fe, NM)

"O Mystery, be exalted beyond word and beyond silence, who became human in order to renew us by means of voluntary union with the flesh. Reveal to me the path by which I may be raised up to your mysteries, traveling along a course that is clear and tranquil, free from the illusions of this world. Gather my mind into the silence of prayer, so that wandering thoughts may be silenced within me during that luminous converse of supplication and mystery-filled wonder" (St Isaac the Syrian).

When we think about the task of growth to spiritual maturity, of being transformed and transfigured in the renewal of our minds, as Paul says in Romans 12—the transfiguration of our being and the renewal of our *nous*—it's a great mystery of salvation, of how God works with us and how we work with God, because it's always mutual. As the saying goes, you get out of it what you put into it. It's the same in the spiritual life. It takes a tremendous amount of effort on our part in order to constantly engage God, constantly be present to God, constantly maintain that awareness of God, and it's a struggle.

It's a struggle, because the things in our lives in the world are distractions. St Isaac has yet another wonderful prayer, which puts things into perspective:

I beg of you, Lord, do not set against me the sins of my youth, the ignorance of my old age, and the frailty of my nature, which is too

55

strong for me and has caused me to sink into reflection on things that are hateful. Rather, turn my heart towards you, away from the troublesome distraction of lust. Cause to dwell in me a hidden light. Your acts of goodness towards me always anticipate any kind of volition on my part to do well and any readiness for virtue on the part of my heart.

Our lives in the world are full of distractions. When one enters a monastery, one of the first things noticed is that there are no distractions. No job with co-workers; no TV or radio; no movies or novels; no newspapers or magazines; no music playing in the background as there is everywhere, to keep the soul from confronting itself, to keep one distracted. One of the hardest things for most of us is to be quiet with ourselves. It's hard to sit and simply be silent, because there are so many thoughts and memories and things that just bubble to the surface.

Part of the spiritual life and battle is to learn how to deal with those thoughts, to learn to focus our attention. Keeping our attention centered on the presence of God everywhere at all times is a fundamental ability and power which the grace of God has placed within us. When we're in a state of distraction in the world, our attention is going off all different directions. St Isaac the Syrian says this is like a shameless bird going off and getting into all sorts of things. So the real core of our ascetic task is to learn to focus our attention on God. It's very difficult at first, but then it gets easier and easier, once you've dealt with the issues that arise.

It's important to know how the Holy Fathers understand the human person. Though it is part of the common tradition of the East and the West, it was later buried in the West and lost entirely with the Reformation. A whole different understanding of the human person has evolved since the Reformation and the so-called "Enlightenment." I say "so-called" because in reality, our whole culture plunged into great spiritual darkness during this time.

The human person was created with two centers of consciousness: One is the rational mind, which includes the emotions. The other is the heart, otherwise known in Greek terminology as the *nous*. There's no good English translation for nous. The Latin translation, which would be used in our English translations of the Latin Fathers, is only confusing in our contemporary idiom, because the word used is "intellectus." We think the intellect is the head. But in fact, it is the traditional Latin translation for the word nous.

The concept of the nous is distinct from our rational perception, and rational perception is how we process all the information that comes in from our senses—from sight, hearing, smell, taste, touch, how we reason, how we understand things, how we look at things. In a sense, it's a secondary kind of reasoning, because it relies completely on our perceptions through our senses, whereas our noetic understanding, our noetic vision, our noetic awareness, is direct perception.

In our terminology, the very definition of the Fall is the clouding and obscuring of our noetic perception, and the elevation of our rational understanding as the primary way we perceive the world. Now we're living entirely in our heads. Depending on our circumstances, our environment and how we've been raised, our noetic perception is, to varying degrees, blinded.

This is our state of fallenness. It introduces into us not only a brokenness in our ability to perceive God, which is what our noetic perception is, because the nous itself is the very image of God within us. Our state of fallenness also keeps us separated from one another, because we perceive ourselves and others as autonomous individuals.

Autonomous individuality, or individualism, means defining ourselves in distinction over against other people. It is the very nature of fallenness. This poisonous kind of individualism is a dangerous tendency in American culture, and powerful forces in our society tend to exalt it. In opposition to this tendency, we Orthodox Christians are called to love and communion, as our very salvation depends upon our relationships with our brothers and sisters.

Our task of being fulfilled in love and communion, indeed, all the rest of our spiritual life, depends on opening that noetic eye, the eye of our heart.

There's another possible confusion here. Most often we think of the heart in terms of emotions. As Americans, this is our idiom. "Oh, I feel it in my heart," means "I feel it with my emotions." No. In spiritual terminology, the "heart" has nothing to do with the emotions. The emotions are in your head. The emotions are how your body feels, which you process rationally with your mind and put into words.

Remember that the word nous in Latin is "intellectus". The term for noetic perception in Latin is "intuition." Intuition has many different levels, among them the popular idea of women's intuition as opposed to men's rational approach. There's a point to that, but the real intuition in this sense is the awareness of our noetic consciousness and its discernment of right and wrong, good and evil. It is direct. It's not about having to think about it. It's not about some kind of decision by discursive logic: "Oh, it has these good points; it has these bad points. I'll weigh the pros and cons."

This kind of reasoning or rational thought is what the Holy Fathers, in particular St Maximos the Confessor, call the gnomic will. The gnomic will is the autonomous will, self-will, of a fallen individual. At the monastery, we sometimes joke that someone is being gnomic, and one of the brothers has a little statue of a garden gnome as an illustration.

The gnomic will is our will as it's processed through our heads and our emotions, completely autonomously of everybody else, including God. In distinction to that, the Fathers talk about having a natural will, who and what we were made to be in the image of God. It's only through overcoming that autonomous self-will, the gnomic will, and opening up to God and then reintegrating our whole being and our whole life in Him through the nous, that we return to communion with God and neighbor in love.

If we're solely defining ourselves in terms of our own individuality and our own distinction from other people, where is the love? There might be like, and there might be dislike. There might be hatred, but there's no love. And love is itself the very energy of God poured into our soul through our noetic perception, through our intuition, which is a participation in the love of God.

With love, we no longer define ourselves simply in terms of "I'm different from him, and I'm different from her, and I'm different from them, and I'm different from . . . "—but rather, my personhood is defined only in the relationship of love with God and with one another. The more we purify ourselves, the more we can overcome that autonomous individuality which results from living completely in our head instead of being informed by the conscious awareness of God, which comes from our heart as the intuitive awareness of our noetic faculty.

To the degree that we can cleanse and purify ourselves of that autonomy, then to that degree, we're freer to love. And we are freer not only to love the other, but to become authentically the person that God has created us to be: A person in communion, defined by communion and by the relationship of love with one another, and the relationship of love with God. There is an emotional aspect to love, but love far transcends any emotional expression and is not governed by our emotions. It's the inner nature of our relationship with one another.

When I visited Elder Isaaki on Valaam a couple of years ago he described this process as the expansion of our personal "I." As we grow and overcome the egocentrism of defining ourselves totally in terms of our own perceptions and understanding, feelings, and thoughts, our authentic self emerges and embraces not only us but all of those around us.

The mystery of marriage is that the couple is one mystical person in Christ. A monastery is the analogous sacrament; but instead of being married to one person, you're married to a dozen or more. That's really challenging! The point is that our "I" expands so that "I" no longer means me. "I" includes the whole brotherhood. I can't conceive of myself without the brotherhood, without Dimitri and Martin and John and Cyril and Joshua and the rest of the brothers. They're me. It's my "I."

The more we purify ourselves, the more our "I" expands. It embraces the whole parish, embraces all the spiritual children, embraces the whole Church, embraces the whole nation. These are the saints. Ultimately, the "I" of Jesus in his humanity embraced the whole creation.

This is what Father Sophrony calls the hypostatic principle: That the mystery of our being, of our existence, as St Paul says, is hidden with Christ in God (Col 3:3), as Jesus prayed, "that they may be one, Father, as we are one, I in them and thou in me, that they may be perfectly one" (John 17:21–22). This is the great mystery of our union in Christ as one mystical person.

You see, being a Christian is not merely being a follower of Jesus. Being a Christian means to be so completely united in the Son to the Father by the Holy Spirit that in Jesus it even transcends a "we." It becomes an "I" embracing all of creation. As the Church, we come before the Father, offering ourselves to Christ, ourselves in Christ and Christ in us as one mystical person in the ultimate self-offering of love, which is the Eucharist. It's all fulfilled in the Holy Mysteries, in the Eucharist. Our life as Christians is constantly renewed, reaffirmed, and actualized by receiving the body of Christ and entering into Christ's own self-offering to the Father. When we partake of the Holy Mysteries, we become one in Christ with the Father.

"So that the world," as Jesus continued, "might know that the Father has sent Jesus." Our spiritual task as Orthodox Christians is to enter into and to make this mystical reality, of our union in Christ with the Father by the Holy Spirit, the conscious, foundational reality of every aspect of our lives. As the Word of God came and took on our humanity, became everything that we are, so He has enabled us by the grace of the Holy Spirit to become everything that He is. We live as Jesus did, with the mind of Christ, in that overwhelming awareness of the presence of Father.

Question and Answer Session

You talk about this expansion of the personal "I," the oneness of being, of identity, that we strive towards. At the same time, isn't the paradox that God does give each one of us a name; and that's the paradox of the Trinity too, one God, yet still three distinct persons?

+Jonah: A unity of being and a multiplicity of persons. And the unity of being is not compromised by the multiplicity, nor is the personal integrity compromised by the unity. The Father, the Son, and the Holy

Spirit, forever remain distinct, yet completely interpenetrate one another.

The same is true among us. In being fragmented into autonomous individuals, we are compromised into egocentric atoms. It compromises our unity as persons.

The task is not, is not to lose our personhood, but to actualize our personhood by our unity with one another. And thus not only is our unity fulfilled, but our personhood becomes fulfilled—in other words, we become who God made us to be. Not what. Who.

And that is a mystery hidden with Christ in God (Col 3:3). We can never rationally comprehend it. People in their early twenties are often said to be searching for identity. Well, the mystery is that you'll never be able to define yourself, because as soon as you do define yourself, it's a false self.

So am I understanding that the unity that we see between the Father, Son, and the Holy Spirit is the same unity that we should be striving for as mankind, to be one?

+Jonah: Yes. We're united in the Son by the Holy Spirit to the Father, and we partake of the Son's union with the Father by the Holy Spirit. And so our personhood, our interrelationship with one another in love, becomes the sacrament, the mystery, of our union in Christ with the Father by the Spirit.

The Church, for example, is composed of sacramental communities: marriage, monasticism, the Church as community actualized in the Eucharist in the bond of love. It is a manifestation here and now, in this reality, in this world, of that ultimate eschatological union of all in Christ by the Holy Spirit with the Father.

Trinitarian theology is essential and fundamental to who we are as Orthodox Christians. We can't understand ourselves as Christians without the Trinity. It's how we relate to God. Our experience of God is the Trinity. We relate to God as Father because we have been given the gift of the Holy Spirit to enable us to share the sonship of Jesus.

Now, yes, we're all sons and daughters of God, but it is Jesus' relation of Sonship that we share with the Father by grace.

When you start losing your "false self" is it normal to feel like it is compromising your personhood?

+Jonah: That's a really important stage. In the spiritual life, one of the most important things is that the further you go forward, the more it feels like you're losing ground and going backwards. All of these issues rise up, and all the ways you've defined yourself, and all the ways that you'd understood yourself, certainly all the ways that you'd understood God and everything else, has to go. This is hard, but it's essential. It's fundamental to the whole process.

I was wondering how obedience works in the expanding of one's self?

+Jonah: Well, if it's just my will as an autonomous individual that the monks are being obedient to, there may be some value to obedience for training and for cutting off their wills. But obedience is essential to the Christian life, not just in monasticism. Two of the things that we have to remember as Orthodox Christians are that our whole lives as Christians are about obedience, and that there is no Christianity without asceticism.

In Orthodox Christianity, there is no Jesus without the cross. Jesus said, "He who would follow me must deny himself daily and take up his cross and follow me" (Mt 16:24). That is asceticism. Now, what that asceticism is, depends on your circumstances. Obedience has to be present, not only in the monastery, but in marriage. That's not a popular thing to say. There's a *taxis*, an order, and there has to be a mutual obedience.

Father Christopher and I were joking the other day. We were observing that it's not as if the abbot isn't obedient to anybody. The abbot is obedient to the whole community. The abbot has to keep everyone in mind and their needs—their strengths and their weaknesses—in order to be able to give the obediences to the rest of the community and for it to work as a whole.

It does work as an organic whole. The abbot is the sacrament of the presence of Christ in the midst of the community, as the husband is the sacrament of Christ, the presence of Christ, in the midst of a marriage, as a priest is the sacrament of the presence of Christ in a Eucharistic community.

There is to be an "orderly arrangement," a *taxis* that doesn't diminish in any way, shape, or form any other member of the community. This is not about some kind of patriarchal domination. It's about responsibility in Christ to be the one who holds all together in love.

It must be emphasized: Christian obedience has absolutely nothing to do with a military style of regimentation and discipline. Discipline is good and important and necessary, but real obedience means communion in love. When we keep in mind that real obedience is about communion, cooperation, synergy in love, then the rebellion and everything else that is in us dissipates. Obedience itself is a sacrament of grace.

A monastery is the sacrament of obedience. It is a holy mystery that holds it together as that living communion in love. Marriage is the same thing. I think maybe because we've lost sight of that, many marriages are in chaos.

How should you proceed in a worldly situation where there is not the mutual goal of love among everyone? Certainly, a person would want to love in an Orthodox way in a worldly situation as well.

+Jonah: That's the task. But, we have to be aware of our own strength and of the strength of our own spiritual perception. Most of us don't have the strength to love unconditionally those who are enemies and those who hate us and persecute us. That strength comes from God. It means that we have a lot more work to do. I live in Marin County. A lot of people think of it as a crazy place. One weekend there were protesters on the Hub, a big intersection in the area. Their signs said, "We hate Bush," and "End the war," and "Bring them home," and so on.

Somebody got up there with a big sign that said, "Jesus said, Love your enemies." The other protesters said it was too radical. "You can't say love your enemies. It's just too much." It would mean they would have to love George Bush, and so that doesn't work for them.

Father, as you said, we're dealing with a technical language, and maybe you could spend just a moment longer on a definition of obedience? I think it's easy for Americans to think that obedience means doing what somebody tells you to do. I've read in Orthodoxy the idea of the members of a family being obedient to each other. When my son comes to me and says, "Dad, will you please make me dinner?" in effect I say, "Oh, okay, I'll extend obedience to you. I'll make you dinner." But if he comes to me half an hour before dinner, and says, "Dad, will you please give me some ice cream?" in that case, I'll seem to break this communion of obedience because I'm not giving him what he wants. I think the idea of obedience is that we want what's best for somebody.

+Jonah: Exactly. And the person in the position of responsibility bears that responsibility to discipline. You know, the Lord disciplines those whom He loves. Of course, one would say sometimes, "Lord, why do you have to love us so much?"

Discipline is hard. I find as an abbot it's one of the hardest things that I have to do, to discipline the brothers. It's not about a power trip. If it is about the power trip, I'm in the wrong business. So within that structure of communion and love, there is always order; there's always the person in the role of responsibility.

Jean Vanier, a French Catholic who is a brilliant contemporary theologian, founded L'Arche Houses. These communities take in people with disabilities, and they also take in young people, purportedly to work with the people with disabilities, but the reality is, it's the people with disabilities who are working with the young people to help them mature and grow.

I've seen him billed in the press as a contemporary Mother Teresa. He's written a brilliant book called *Community and Growth*, which talks about the gift of authority as responsibility. Authority takes on a whole different dimension if you understand it this way. It's not authority over people. It's authority within, and it's responsibility for the sake of the whole in love. Isn't this the mind of the Church? Isn't this really what it is? Responsibility for the whole in love, in obedience to the whole.

Having that catholic mind, having that mind of the wholeness of our unity in Christ by the Holy Spirit as one person, how can we dare to rebel or offend one another? When we're doing that, it sets us apart not only from one another, but from God.

St Isaac has a wonderful prayer:

> I knock at the door of your compassion, Lord. Send aid to my scattered impulses, which are intoxicated with the multitude of the passions and the power of darkness. You can see my sores hidden within me. Stir up contrition though not corresponding to the weight of my sins, for if I receive full awareness of the extent of my sins, Lord, my soul would be consumed by the bitter pain from them.

Our sin is our separation from one another and all that separates us from one another and all that separates us from God. The core of that, the root of that sinfulness, is our false self.

I think part of the struggle is that we want definitions. But there's not a list of dos and don'ts. Instead it's an extension of how open your nous is in dealing with each situation personally.

+Jonah: Right. We want it black and white. We want it easily, nicely done on paper. I need to do this, this, and this. I should not do this, this, and this. And if I do those things, I need to go to confession so that I can assuage my conscience. That's the lowest level of spiritual development.

The deeper you get into the spiritual life, the less definition there is. That's how St Paul can say, "All things are lawful for me" (1 Cor 6:12). Think of the freedom that it takes to be able to say that. "All things are lawful for me."

It blows our whole rational understanding, but that's the point. When we're caught up in our rational minds and our autonomous individuality, we're caught up in our ego and our false selves, the selves that we have created—not that God has created! We create our false selves by our passions and by our false expectations.

We create the false self by what others think of us and how we want them to think of us and how we have succeeded and how we have failed and on and on. We get caught up in this whole idea of who and what we are and how things should be. It's completely limited by our own perceptions, by what other people think of us, what we think other people think of us, whether I succeeded and did well or did poorly, all of this.

St Paul categorizes this in I Corinthians chapter two, into the schema of being "carnal" (or "natural"), and "spiritual." He says the natural man does not receive the things of the Spirit. The word he uses for "natural" is *psychikos*. He doesn't mean psychic in the sense of Madame So-and-So, the Palm Reader—that's something else. Most of us live most of the time on the carnal and psychic levels. Carnal is self-explanatory, but psychic means "of the soul," which means the rational and the emotional, the desiring, and the capacity for anger etc., the "works of the flesh" in Galatians chapter 5.

Then we have to talk about how those things get played out. How those things get played out is called the passions. The passions are ways of acting that have become so habitual that they become short circuits for us. When a thought comes into our mind that keys off one of our passions, we immediately go down the slippery slope right into a fall into the passions.

When we try to come to terms with our false selves and to figure out how to move out of this morass of being trapped in our heads, the place where the rubber meets the road is in how we deal with our thoughts. Our thoughts include feelings and emotions, which are just a different aspect of rational perception. The technical term for all that is *logismoi*, thoughts. The thoughts are in our heads, right?

When we get wrapped up in a thought, it pulls our attention away from God. Think about standing in church and trying to pray. All of a sudden, a thought comes in, and we may have been pretty focused on prayer, but then all of a sudden we're thinking about, "Oh, what's for dinner?" We're thinking about something entirely different, which has nothing to with the Liturgy.

The battle with the thoughts is the real place where we begin to struggle with our true selves and our false selves. Our true selves can emerge only when we can focus our attention on the presence of God and reintegrate our whole life according to the grace that pours forth through that, rather than living with our thoughts dispersed and our attention dispersed according to all the things of this world.

Initially I talked about distractions. What are distractions? They're things that capture our attention and provoke distracted thoughts. I think we all know perfectly well that we can be sitting alone in a silent, dark room and we'll still have a multitude of thoughts, just as if there were a TV on and a movie playing and the radio blasting.

One of the best ways of thinking about thoughts is that they're like ads for the passions. We need to learn to use the mute button, but not only the mute button. We need to learn how to turn it off. That battle is the real meat of our spiritual lives. What do we do with these random thoughts that come into our minds?

I want to make clear that I'm not talking about discursive reasoning, which can be good and important. It has a place. There's an order within us, and discursive reasoning and thought, when we engage in it in a focused way, is incredibly valuable. But it has to be subordinate to the awareness of God, the remembrance of God.

In striving to keep our awareness of God focused, we need to learn how to deal with these random thoughts that come to distract us from that awareness of God. One thing that we easily fall into is trying to battle with them. I can almost guarantee you that unless you're on a very high level of spiritual accomplishment, if you try to battle with your thoughts, you're going to lose. The point is not to battle with the thoughts; it's to let them go by.

Most of us have learned how to ignore a TV or a stereo or a conversation going on in the next room. You don't have to enter in. You don't have to listen to it. It's the same thing with our thoughts. You don't have to listen to them. You can let them go by, like birds outside the window.

It takes a lot of practice, and this is the real essence of asceticism. Asceticism is not about fasting yourself skinny, wearing prayer ropes, and doing hundreds of prostrations and all of that. Sometimes all that does is feed your vainglory, your passions. Self-directed asceticism is one of the most harmful things in the spiritual life, especially for people who are immature, like me.

Asceticism is the practice of self-denial and the practice of denying ourselves our thoughts. It's saying no to our self and cutting off the thoughts. Very often we think we're going to derive pleasure from our thoughts. Maybe we have a lustful thought, and then we engage in it, and then . . . we all know the process. There may be gratification, but there's no fulfillment. There's no gratification in self-gratification. There's no fulfillment, and there's certainly no joy.

It doesn't matter what kind of thought it is. It may be lustful, avaricious, despairing. A lot of people don't understand that despondency and despair are passions and can be dealt with in the same way as lust or pride or avarice or jealousy or envy or anything else. All the passions work the same way.

A thought comes into our mind, and our mind decides to play with it, to examine it. Then we start to kind of engage it. And if we have a long-established habitual reaction to that thought, it's a slippery slope, and we go right down into a sin. Before we even know it, we engage it, and then we agree with the thought and then we make a decision to execute it. And then comes the actual commission of the act. All the passions work the same way, but each has its own little peculiarities.

How we engage the thought and how we watch over our thoughts, to the extent that we are watchful over our thoughts, and stop ourselves from engaging thoughts that we know will to lead us into sin is the real task of asceticism. That's where we can stop our sinful actions and attitudes and even habits of mind, all of which constitute the false self.

CHAPTER 4

Purifying Our True Selves

(Adapted from an Audio Transcript of a Retreat given in Santa Fe, NM)

+Jonah: I'd like to make a couple of concluding comments on this discussion of thoughts and spirituality. Most of our time is spent in our heads, distracted. It's important for each one of us to look at the things that keep us in our heads. In other words, on the psychological (remember, *psychikós*) level, we have to move from psychology to spirituality, from psychological religion into authentic spirituality. Authentic spirituality is noetic consciousness. That's where spirituality begins.

Before true spirituality, you have religion. You have the dos and the don'ts and all the words. Words are important, but we have to ask where they are coming from. Are they coming just from the head? Or are they informed by that noetic vision?

There's a stage beyond noetic vision. It's what the Fathers call *theología*—theology—mystical communion with God. I can guarantee you that most of what passes for theology in our culture has absolutely nothing to do with *theología*. It has much more to do with publish and perish. Academic theology, for the most part, is not about mystical perception of God.

Theología, the mystical perception of God, is beyond any rational awareness. This may sound kind of New Agey, but it's not. In a sense we're talking about a growth and a transformation of our consciousness.

When we're living in our heads, all we're aware of is what our senses can perceive. It's like a two-dimensional reality. So we tend to say, "Unless it's written down in black and white, I won't believe it. Unless I can touch it, unless I can feel it, unless I can observe it scientifically, it can't be true. Unless it's written in the *Rudder* and is a canon of the Church, unless we do everything according to the *Typicon* of the Church, it's not a valid Liturgy. He left out a troparion; we have to start over."

This is all in the head. What's important is to grow beyond all of this stuff. As our consciousness expands and our minds and our hearts become more and more integrated and purified, then we move into what the Fathers call natural contemplation.

Here again, in the way we think about "theology," people want to go right from academic theology into mystical union. It doesn't work that way. What's happening through asceticism is a gradual sanctification and illumination, the enlightenment of our souls. Along with that, and as a byproduct of that, is control of our thoughts and our passions.

Apáthia, dispassion, is the Buddhist definition of enlightenment. The idea of enlightenment is dispassion, so that you're completely free of thoughts, or you can still the thoughts and directly perceive reality. When we directly perceive reality with an illumined mind, with a mind not only enlightened by dispassion, which cannot come through our own efforts, but by the grace of the Holy Spirit, all of creation becomes radiant with the presence of God. All of creation becomes luminous and transparent in God.

I think this is what St Paul is talking about when he says at the beginning of Romans, "For since the creation of the world, his invisible attributes are clearly seen, being understood by the things that are made, even His eternal power and Godhead" (Rom 1:20). If our minds were clear, the eternal power and presence of God would be radiantly visible, not just with our physical eyes, but with the noetic eyes of our hearts, so that all of creation sings the glory of God.

And from there, by the grace of God and the sanctification of our souls, imagine if we could view other people from a state of natural contemplation, *theoría physikí*. We would see the radiant presence of God in each person. We would see that each person is a living icon of God, filled with God's image and likeness. Believer, unbeliever, Orthodox, Catholic, Buddhist, Hindu, atheist, everyone, every human person is a radiant image of God. What then can you do but love?

Beyond that is *theología*. This is what God is calling us to. This is not something that's only for monks or people who are living a completely ascetic life. The Gospel was not given just to the monks. It's for every one of us. What is given to the monks is given to every one of us, if we take it.

So with that, I'll open up to questions.

Question and Answer Session

I've lived in Taos this year, and I've had to understand distinctions between some New Age teachings and our faith. Many people talk about Christ consciousness. I don't think that's what you're saying, but I'd like to try to add to the distinction by saying that I do think Orthodoxy will change our consciousness. Prayer changes our consciousness. One of the things that came to me is that God is a person first and we're involved with a person first. Changing consciousness seems to me to be a great by-product. When the first Christians were being fed to the lions, they didn't do so to change their consciousness. They did so out of love for God. My wife, Thecla, changes my consciousness, but that's not why I'm with her. I agree that there's an analogy between our concept of illumination and the Buddhist concept of enlightenment, but neither enlightenment nor illumination is yet theosis, I don't think.

+Jonah: He's right.

A monk told me that he was a former Hindu and explained Christian mystical experience this way: In Christian mystical experience one could be seen as a drop in the ocean, but the drop remains a drop and the ocean remains the ocean. The person doesn't just dissipate and become the ocean.

+Jonah: Right. The personal integrity of the each one is maintained. That's God's great gift of grace. Any mystical experience is actually a participation in the kingdom which is to come. There's the so-called enlightenment of dispassion, but the real enlightenment—Christian enlightenment—is the illumination of the soul by the Holy Spirit, which is the process of deification.

You can have dispassion by human discipline. There are many, many ascetics who have—Buddhists, Taoists, Hindus, and so on. For them it is a discipline of learning how to cut off the thoughts and cut off the passions.

We have help, and that help is powered by our repentance, because it's a constant turning of our attention towards God. This focuses on contemplative prayer. There's a big difference between Buddhist meditation and contemplative prayer. Buddhism is essentially a humanist philosophy. It's a philosophy like other philosophies and can be syncretized and combined with all sorts of other things. It's a philosophy of learning to be quiet and focus your mind and overcome your passions and that sort of thing.

The point is, that for Christians, the Holy Spirit is active within us by grace. The activity of the Holy Spirit is working, joining with us, and we intentionally unite our efforts with the work of the Holy Spirit, so that it's not simply some kind of a human state of awareness, but rather it's an awareness that's in the Holy Spirit. It's not seeing God in all things; rather, it's seeing all things in God, so that our awareness is illumined by the very presence of God.

The highest state of prayer is the Holy Spirit praying within us, being aware that the Holy Spirit is praying within us. It's not a rational awareness at all, but a noetic awareness, so it's a deified perception of all things in the Holy Spirit. It's a radical distinction from any kind of human philosophical practice.

The transformation of consciousness is what happens to us as we engage in the spiritual life. We don't do it to transform our consciousness. Well, we might. It's good to want deification. It's good to want salvation, which is deification. The two things are synonymous. But to engage in spiritual discipline for a self-serving end is a very subtle kind of egocentrism, and it produces spiritual pride and vainglory, and it gets us nowhere. We think we're really advanced, but instead, we're even more fallen. One of the things about the higher levels of spirituality, is that the temptations become much more subtle.

As I try to sort this into nice little definitions that I can manage, it sounds to me as if the work of cutting off our thoughts so that we're not distracted is the work that human beings do. But the end result is in some sense a vacuum that has to be filled by something, and the question is, "What?" Somehow or other, filling of that vacuum is going to be God's work, God's energies, God's grace, but somehow or other there's a piece that says God wants to do that, but there's another piece that says, am I going to let Him do it or am I going to let some other thing fill that space?

+Jonah: The whole point is that it's our willingness to enter into cooperation with God. Otherwise, it's like the parable of Jesus, when He cast out the demon, who then comes back and finds the house swept and put in order but empty, and brings seven more with it (Mt 12:45). One of the great tasks in this is confronting those very subtle areas where we don't want to let God in, where we don't want to repent. Here repentance also has a kind of different meaning, different content, according to the level you're talking about.

The first level of repentance is to stop doing bad things. The next level is to stop thinking bad thoughts and turn toward God. Turning toward God is implied in the first level, but the first level is focused mostly on not doing bad things, because they make me feel guilty. It's still about me, and it's still all in the head.

At the next level, we have the beginning of an awareness of God. We become more watchful over our thoughts, and we're learning how to cut them off, but then we have to confront those thoughts that we don't really want to cut off. This is where resentments are really important, resentments and remembrance of wrongs, because we feel justified in being angry at people and maintaining resentments for people who've hurt us.

Another essential aspect of this whole process is forgiveness. More and more we confront ourselves and see these areas in ourselves that we don't want to let go of, but then we can will to let go, because these are areas where we're out of synergy. We're outside of cooperation with God; we're refusing to cooperate with God.

If we're just doing it on our own, we're not going to get very far. These principles are present in the Twelve Step programs such as Alcoholics Anonymous, because AA has come from basic patristic spirituality. AA calls participants to surrender themselves to their higher power, however they understand it. And this formulation is very good, by the way, because initially, people are caught up in their own heads, into their own understanding of God. It takes a long time before we can simply surrender to the God who is and stand at the abyss. And it is an abyss.

This whole spiritual task is all process. There's nothing concrete. There's no way that you can say at any point, "I've arrived." That's difficult. No sooner do we figure out this area that I've finally willed to be able to surrender to God, than He'll show me another one. This is where synergy comes in. Synergy is cooperation with divine grace and with God's active presence and involvement in our spiritual paths and tasks.

It's profoundly personal. God is not just some abstract power. We can think of divine energy as some abstract power, but that's not it at all. It's God's personal involvement in our life that shows us and illumines these areas in which we need to repent, in which we need to surrender to God.

What comes to mind is an explanation, a description of the white stone from the Book of Revelation, by George MacDonald. In that book, MacDonald says that each person in the womb is given a secret name, and in the process of his life, the person will not know his own name until he becomes that person God intended. MacDonald is describing deification.

+Jonah: Amen. That's it exactly. In a sense, the whole spiritual quest is to find our name, which is absolutely unique to us through all eternity, by the grace of God.

In light of all you've said, how does a person deal with doubt and trust?

+Jonah: Doubt and belief go together, but belief and faith are two different things. Belief is in your head; faith is in your heart. Faith is noetic awareness. That's what's given by the Holy Spirit at baptism. Belief is how we process that.

Part of how we process that is through asking questions and through doubt. I think we all know that we could have all sorts of doubts, but our faith remains solid. That faith is the noetic intuition of the reality of God.

The mystery of holy illumination—of baptism and chrismation—is constantly renewed in confession and through partaking of the Holy Mysteries. That is the divine opening of the noetic eye of our heart, so that we can see God, which is faith.

That whole scheme of purification, illumination, deification comes from the Holy Fathers' writings about baptism. Hierotheos Vlachos has written a lot about the subject.

Purification is what the catechumenate is about. It's not about learning all sorts of facts about the Church and all sorts of laws and how to fast. It is that, too, and it helps, but it's not the point. It's our process of our purification as we prepare to receive the holy mystery of illumination, which is a gift of God, by grace, in baptism and chrismation, that we might be deified by partaking of the Lord's Body and Blood.

This is all a sacramental vision of the Holy Fathers and then the later Fathers. The ascetic Fathers took this same schema of purification, illumination, and deification to describe growth in the spiritual life, because it is repeated again and again, because again and again we have to repent and recommit ourselves to Christ. How many times do we say in the Liturgy, "Again and again, let us commit ourselves and each other and all our life unto Christ our God"?

These are not empty words, even though we say them over and over. It's to remind us that the process is constant and ongoing and that our surrender to Christ and our conversion and our repentance and committing ourselves to Christ is not just done once in our life. It's not just at a few key times. It's not even just going up to the altar call once a month at the revival meeting. It's several times even just during the time the Liturgy is taking place!

It's this task that we're all engaged in, and that's why every Orthodox Christian is a convert. We're all Orthodox by choice, not by chance. Even if we've been born and raised in the faith and had it handed to us from our youth on a silver platter, we still have to take it. We still have to take it and make it our own, and the only way that we can be a Christian is by repentance. There's no salvation by association. It's only by repentance and being actively engaged in this spiritual battle, in the arena of spiritual life.

You mention choice not chance, and it brings to mind the question of how our own free will works here. If that eye starts to open just a crack even, and you start to feel that work happen, I'm wondering if the dynamic that starts to play out is that, yes, there's faith and faith in God that God won't abandon us. It seems that the more troubling doubt can be doubt in your own ability. As you said, our sin is the barriers we erect between ourselves and God. If that crack starts to open, perhaps you recognize, "Oh, well God will meet that." How can you help the doubt that no matter where you might be in the process at that time, you will certainly put up another barrier, and perhaps close the door?

+Jonah: The real problem is not God. God's love is absolute, and His forgiveness is absolute and unconditional. His love, His forgiveness, His mercy, His compassion are absolute and unconditional, constant, eternal. God is not waiting to damn us for the least little slip, for having whey in our protein bars or the cookie that we ate surreptitiously. That notion is a false God that we've created out of our own fallen, broken, sick minds, because we don't perceive Him.

One of the things that's the hardest is that we need to forgive ourselves for our sins. God forgives us our sins; it's we who hang onto them. We make ourselves feel guilty; we condemn ourselves. In fact, God does not condemn us to hell. God's judgment is His mercy, His compassion, His love, His forgiveness. It's we that condemn ourselves to hell when we reject it because we think, "I'm unworthy."

Yes, I'm unworthy. Is my response to that unworthiness to reject the mercy and compassion and love of God because it's a burning coal heaped on my head when I know that I constantly reject God? How can I accept it, when I refuse to forgive myself and I refuse to accept God's forgiveness?

St Isaac the Syrian, again, one of my favorite Fathers, has an incredibly powerful image of hell. Hell is being immersed in the love of God. One of the reasons the Orthodox Church rejects purgatory and created hellfire is that we say, "No, it's not created. It's uncreated. It's God's uncreated energy, his uncreated love, which we reject, which burns us because we hate it and reject it."

By refusing to believe that I can be forgiven and refusing to accept God's love and compassion and forgiveness, I refuse by my own will to forgive myself. We have a rather different approach to condemnation. Otherwise, God is a tyrant, and who needs that God? It's not the God of the Scriptures. It's not the God of Jesus Christ. It's not the God of the Fathers.

It's God's infinite mercy and compassion and His love for us that allows us even to reject Him, maintaining our existence by His love and by His joy, even if we hate it, even if it torments us because He loves so much and wants us to exist unto all eternity, because He wants to be in relationship with us.

Our God is a consuming fire, and it's a fearful thing to fall into the hands of the living God, as Hebrews says (Heb 10:31). It's a fearful thing, because either we'll be ignited with that radiant joy and deified and glow with that same radiance, or in refusing it, will be burned by it. He respects us—our autonomy, our personhood, our true selves!

Heaven and hell are the same thing. It's our attitude toward them that makes it heaven or makes it hell. I'm not just talking about after death; I'm talking about right now.

CHAPTER 5

Do Not Resent; Do Not React; Keep Inner Stillness

THE THREE FUNDAMENTAL PRINCIPLES OF SPIRITUAL LIFE

(AGAIN Vol. 28 No. 1, Spring 2006)

When we consider how to apply the wisdom of the Church to the struggles of our daily lives, we immediately face difficult questions. How do we go about spiritual growth and transformation? How do we allow God to enter into our lives? How do we surrender ourselves and turn to God in the continual mystery of constant repentance which changes with each successive stage of our spiritual adventure? First, we must acknowledge that the answers to such questions are only revealed as part of a gradual process. This is something which takes years. However, there are certain key principles of the spiritual life which can guide our journey, even from the very beginning.

When I was in seminary I had the great blessing of becoming the spiritual son of a Greek bishop, Bishop Kallistos of Xelon. He ended his life as the bishop of Denver of the Greek Archdiocese. It was he who taught me the Jesus Prayer. The whole spiritual vision of Bishop Kallistos had three very simple points.

Do not resent. Do not react. Keep inner stillness.

These three spiritual principles, or disciplines, are really a summation of the *Philokalia*, the collection of Orthodox Christian spiritual wisdom. And they are disciplines every single one of us can practice, no matter where we are in life—whether we're in the monastery or in school; whether we're housewives or retired; whether we've got a job or we've got little kids to run after. If we can hold on to and exercise these three principles, we will be able to go deeper and deeper in our spiritual life.

Do Not Resent

When we look at all the inner clutter that is in our lives, hearts and souls, what do we find? We find resentments. We find remembrance of wrongs. We find self-justifications. We find these in ourselves because of pride. It is pride that makes us hold on to our justifications for our continued anger against other people. And it is hurt pride, or vainglory, which feeds our envy and jealousy. Avarice is to be more and more consumed with envy, the desire to have what others have. Envy and jealousy lead to resentment.

Resentfulness leads to a host of problems. The more resentful we are of other people, the more depressed we become. Often we'll then engage in the addictive use of the substance of the material world—whether it's food or alcohol or drugs or sex or some other thing—to medicate ourselves into forgetfulness, to distract ourselves from our resentments.

One of the most valuable and important things that we can do in our spiritual life is look at all of the resentments that we have. One of the best ways of accomplishing this is to make a life confession. And not just once, before we're baptized or chrismated. In the course of our spiritual life we may make several, in order to really dig into our past and look at these resentments that we bear against other people. This will enable us to do the difficult work that it takes to overcome these resentments through forgiveness.

What does forgiveness mean? Forgiveness does not mean excusing or justifying the actions of somebody. For example, saying "Oh, he abused me but that's O.K., that's just his nature," or "I deserved it." No, if somebody abused you that was a sin against you. But when we hold resentments, when we hold anger and bitterness within ourselves against those who have abused us in some way, we take their abuse and we continue it against ourselves. We have to stop that cycle. Most likely that person has long gone and long forgotten us, perhaps even forgotten that we even existed; but maybe not. Maybe the abuser was a parent or someone else close, which makes the resentment all the more bitter. But for the sake of our own soul and for the sake of our own peace, we need to forgive. We should not justify the action, but we should look beyond the action and see that there's a person there who is struggling with sin. We should see that the person we have resented, the person we need to forgive, is no different from us, he sins just as we do, and we sin just as he does.

Of course, it helps if the person whom we resent, the person who offended us or abused us in some way, asks forgiveness of us. But we can't wait for this. And we can't hold on to our resentments even after outwardly saying we've forgiven. Think of the Lord's Prayer: "Forgive us our trespasses as we forgive those who trespass against us." If we don't forgive, we can't even pray the Lord's Prayer without condemning ourselves. It's not that God condemns us. We condemn ourselves by refusing to forgive. We will never have peace if we don't forgive, only resentment. It is one of the hardest things to do, and our culture does not understand it. It is to look at the person we need to forgive, and to love them—despite how they may have sinned against us. Their sin is their sin, and they have to deal with it themselves. But our sin is in our reaction against their sin.

Do Not React

So this first spiritual principle—do not resent—leads to the second: Do not react. We must learn to not react. This is just a corrollary of Jesus' teaching in the Sermon on the Mount to "turn the other cheek"

(Matt 5:39, Luke 6:29). When somebody says something hurtful, or somebody does something hurtful, what is it that's being hurt? It's our ego. Nobody can truly hurt us. They might cause some physical pain, or emotional pain. They might even kill our body. But nobody can hurt our true selves. We have to take responsibility for our own actions. Then we can control our reactions.

There are a number of different levels to this principle. On the most blatant level, if someone hits you, don't hit them back. Turn the other cheek—that's the Lord's teaching. Now, this is hard enough. But there is a deeper level still. If somebody hits you and you don't hit them back but you resent them, and you bear anger and hatred and bitterness against them, you've still lost. You have still sinned. You have still broken your relationship with God, because you bear that anger in your heart.

One of the things which is so difficult to come to terms with is the reality that when we bear anger and resentment and bitterness in our hearts, we erect barriers to God's grace within ourselves. It's not that God stops giving us His grace. It's that we say, "No. I don't want it." What is His grace? It is His love, His mercy, His compassion, His activity in our lives. The holy Fathers tell us that each and every human person who has ever been born on this earth bears the image of God undistorted within themselves. In our Tradition there is no such thing as fallen nature. There are fallen persons, but not fallen nature. The implication of this truth is that we have no excuses for our sins. We are responsible for our sins, for the choices we make. We are responsible for our actions, and our reactions. "The devil made me do it" is no excuse, because the devil has no more power over us than we give him. This is hard to accept, because it is really convenient to blame the devil. It is also really convenient to blame the other person, or our past. But, that is also a lie. Our choices are, in the final analysis, our own.

But there is still an even deeper level. This spiritual principle—do not react—teaches us that we need to learn to not react to thoughts. One of the fundamental aspects of this is called "inner watchfulness". This might seem like a daunting task, considering how many thoughts we have. However, our watchfulness does not need to be focused on our thoughts. Our watchfulness needs to be focused on God. We need to maintain the conscious awareness of God's presence. If we can maintain the conscious awareness of His presence, our thoughts will have no power over us. We can, to paraphrase St Benedict, dash our thoughts against the rock of the presence of God (cf. *Rule* of St Benedict, chapter 4). This is a very ancient patristic teaching. We focus our attention on the remembrance of God. If we can do that, not only will our troubling thoughts go away, but so will our reactions, because reactions are about our thoughts. After all, if someone says something nasty to us, how are we reacting? We are reacting first through our thinking, our thoughts, even if we're habitually accustomed to just lashing out after taking offense with some kind of nasty response of our own. But keeping watch over our minds so that we maintain that living communion with God leaves no room for distracting thoughts. It leaves plenty of room if we decide we need to think something through intentionally in the presence of God. But as soon as we engage in something hateful, we close God out. And the converse is true—as long as we maintain our connection to God, we won't be capable of engaging in something hateful. We won't react.

Keep Inner Stillness

The second principle, the second essential foundation of our spiritual life—do not react—leads to the third. This third principle is the practice of inner stillness. The use of the Jesus Prayer is an extremely valuable tool for this. But the Jesus Prayer is a means, not an end. It is a means for entering into deeper and deeper conscious communion. It's a means for us to acquire and maintain the awareness of the presence of God. The prayer developed within the tradition of hesychasm, in the desert and on the Holy Mountain. But hesychasm is not only about the Jesus Prayer. It is about inner stillness and silence.

Inner stillness is not merely an emptiness. It is a focus on the awareness of the presence of God in the depths of our heart. One of the essential things we have to constantly remember is that God is not "out there" someplace. He's not just in the box on the altar. God is everywhere. And God dwells in the depths of our hearts. When we can come to that awareness of God dwelling in the depths of our hearts, and keep our attention focused in that core, thoughts vanish.

How do we do this? In order to enter into deep stillness, we have to have a lot of our issues resolved. We have to have a lot of our anger and bitterness and resentments resolved. We have to forgive. If we don't, we're not going to come to stillness, because the moment we try to enter stillness our inner turmoil is going to come vomiting out. But this is good, actually—painful, but good. Because when we try to enter into stillness and we begin to see the darkness that is lurking in our souls, then we can begin to deal with it. It must be dealt with because it distracts us from trying to be quiet, from trying to say the Jesus Prayer, but that's just part of the process. And it takes time.

To enter stillness, we must learn to pray, because prayer is communion with God. The Fathers talk about three levels of prayer. The first level is oral prayer, where we're saying the prayer with our lips. We may use a prayer rope, saying "Lord Jesus Christ, have mercy on me," or whatever form of the prayer we use. The next level is mental prayer, where we're saying the prayer in our mind. Prayer of the mind—with the Jesus Prayer, with prayer book prayers, with liturgical prayers—keeps our minds focused and helps to integrate us, so that our lips and our mind are in the same place and doing the same thing. We all know that we can be standing in church, or standing at prayer, and we may be mouthing the words with our lips but our mind is thinking about the grocery list. The second level of prayer overcomes this problem, but it is not the final level. The final level of prayer is prayer of the heart. It is here where we encounter God, in the depths of our soul. It is here where we open the eye of our attention, with the intention of being present to God who is present within us. This is the key and the core of the whole process of spiritual growth and transformation.

Our True Selves

As a consequence of leading an actively engaged spiritual life, we're going to come to see more and more of ourselves until we're sick of ourselves, until we're really tired of all the machinations of the "old man" who is desperately trying to hang on as we're desperately trying to crucify him. But this is the task. We have to crucify the old man, which is corrupt with its passions and lusts. We have to crucify the false self we have created by our egos, for there is no salvation for it. Hell is trying to hang on to our false self.

Remember the words of the Lord: "He who would save his life will lose it. And he who loses his life for My sake and the Gospel will save it. For what does it profit a man to gain the whole world and to lose his soul?" (Mark 8:35–36). He is speaking of the false self which we have to crucify. And the best way of doing that is to not engage it, to let it go. We have to recognize that the thoughts that are coming into our minds are not who we are. Descartes led us into this idea that we are our thoughts—"I think therefore I am." Our Tradition says, "No, absolutely not." Who we are in the depths of our being is hidden in Christ, in God. And if there is anything we can identify with our true self, it is most likely our nous, our spirit. But we must also remember that we are whole, integrated beings. The salvation that Jesus wrought is not just of our spirit. It's not just of our mind. It's not just of our soul. We're resurrected from the dead as whole persons, and we will maintain until all eternity the particularity of our unique personhood—body, soul and spirit.

God has created us to share in His life for eternity. He has created us with that potential, a gift given to us which is only actualized by grace. This is the goal of our existence, that the image of God, which is the very foundation of who we are, might be fulfilled in likeness to God. The image of God is the essence of what we are as human persons. But the likeness to God has to be fulfilled through action, through our synergy, through our cooperation with God, through the process of deification. This is the definition of "salvation". This is what our spiritual life is all about. It's about attaining to the likeness of God—living the likeness of God: mercy, compassion, joy, love, peace, patience. The fruits of the Spirit that St Paul talks about are simply the description of a human person who is fulfilled by the grace of God and has attained His likeness. We see in Jesus Christ the most perfect likeness to God. And we see in the saints—most especially in the Mother of God—the maintaining of that synergy with God, which is the fulfillment of human nature. The Mother of God is the one human person in all of history, from Adam until the Second Coming, who fulfilled likeness to God. This is why she is "more honorable than the cherubim, more glorious beyond compare than the seraphim."

Think for a moment of this calling that God has given to us: The potential to ascend higher than the angels, to be seated with Christ at the very right hand of the Father. In Christ we are raised up to the very right hand of the Father. When He comes again, St Paul promises us, we will be like Him, as He is—radiant with the grace of the Holy Spirit, raised from the dead, transfigured, purified, illumined, deified, filled with the life of the Kingdom to come of which we now partake. The spiritual life is about our partaking of the Kingdom of God here, now, in this life, in this world, that we might be filled with His joy.

This essay was adapted from a lecture given by Fr Jonah to a gathering of lay and monastic Orthodox and Roman Catholic Christians at the Pecos Benedictine Monastery of Pecos, New Mexico, in September 2005.

CHAPTER 6

Shame, the Power behind the Passions

(Adapted from Audio Transcript of a Retreat in Inverness, CA)

Shame is a primal, fundamental emotion. It is profoundly useful to think about how shame is related to fear because there is a deep link between the two. Shame is an essential and fundamental emotion which has tremendous impact on the human being. The beginning of shame is tied with the development of our identity. We develop an identity from the sum of the complex of ideas, structures and scenes which we have experienced in the past, and of scripts of how we understand and process those experiences and prepare ourselves for other experiences. That identity is created by our ego, it is the "false self," and it is fundamentally distinct from the true self, which is who we are in the depths of our being—which ultimately is, as the Scriptures tell us, hidden with Christ in God (Col 3:3). That true self, that authentic person that we are, is our noetic consciousness which is the image of God within us. Our noetic consciousness bears the same consciousness that is like God, but in a created way. We are the created image of God, and therefore that which is in us shares in the qualities of God in whose image we are made.

Because we are created in the image of the Trinitarian God, we believe that we have a fundamental need for relationship—that we are created in, by, and for relationship. In our human existence this basic need is met in physical and psychological ways, by being touched and held, by having somebody to relate to in order to establish our identity. Relationships also help us establish our need for differentiation, because again, in our theology each person is unique. There is a need for nurture and to nurture, for affirmation and to affirm. There is also a fundamental need to feel that you have power, that your "will" can be exercised freely—that you can control your own life. All of this has to do with our *nous*, the center of our consciousness, the faculty by which we apprehend God and rightly assess all things, including our selves (I Cor. 2:14ff).

The *nous*, this consciousness, is something very different from our objective ego identity which is our rational and subconscious thoughts about our selves. One aspect of the noetic energy is the faculty of "attention." The "self" is the subject of that attention, and because we are fragmented as human beings, the "self" becomes an objective self that we have created in our minds. What we build when we create this objective identity is a false self, a false subject. It is false not in the sense of bad, but in the sense that it is not authentic, it is not in the depths of its being who and what we are, it is an image of our self that we have created. God created our noetic identity, but it is we who create our ego identity through our experiences and our definition of them, whether they are defined rationally or emotionally. Some of this is by our own active involvement, and some of it is by our passive responses. And this is where the passions are rooted, in the passive responses to our experience, which is physical as well as intellectual and emotional.

So there is a duality within us, but this duality is not evil. The task of the spiritual life is to bring that objective identity under the control and domination of our noetic identity, our true consciousness which is directed toward God. The goal is that everything that we are become a unified, uniform motion toward God. It is the activity of God entering into all of our life, healing the fragmentation, and then being expressed through our physical, emotional, and mental faculties. This is what we were created for, that our whole person be in synergy with God. Synergy is just the Greek word for "working together," which is, in Latin, co-operation.

This task of bringing ourselves into synergy, into harmony, into cooperation with the divine activity, with the divine will, is a matter of first re-establishing our focus on God. We must strive to keep that focus on God, and to bring the rest of our mind, our heart, our soul, our actions, our feelings and our emotions under control and into that synergy. The experience of shame can be a healthy indicator of how we have failed to cooperate with God in whose image we are created, or it can be an ego reaction of the false self in which we objectively define our self as worthless and hopeless, and because of which we fall into emotional despondency or despair.

So, the beginning of shame happens through a variety of ways. Part of shame is the sense of exposure and nakedness. A good definition of shame might be, "Exposure when we're not ready for it." The reaction of shame, whichever way it comes to us from external sources, creates a whole movement within our selves of withdrawal into ourselves, of withdrawing from communion both with God and with one another.

I mentioned healthy shame. Healthy shame is very, very important, and guilt can be healthy too. But there's healthy guilt and there's toxic guilt and there's healthy shame and toxic shame. Guilt is the feeling of being ashamed about an action. If an action was wrong or inappropriate, well, we all know what guilt feels like. The difference between the feeling of guilt that an action was wrong, and toxic shame, is that with shame there is the thought and feeling that, "I am wrong, I am bad, I am defective, I am garbage, I am worthless." It might be triggered by a wrong action, but then as we process it, we turn it against ourselves, and it is no longer our actions that are wrong, but our very existence— our total person—is bad. And so what emerges is, after a repeated experience of shame, it becomes internalized and defines our self. When this has happened we don't even necessarily need an external experience to feel shame. If you have a kid who is continually told that he's stupid, pretty soon he's going to begin to believe it, and when he does something which doesn't measure up to his self-created standards or some else's standards, he's going to beat himself up. He doesn't need anyone to degrade him and tell him he's stupid, he's going to tell himself he's stupid and he'll drive himself down. This is self-blame or self-contempt which creates a whole toxic system within our selves.

This "toxic system" of shame and self-contempt is set in motion within our families. It begins if we have an emotion, say anger, or a drive, like hunger or sex, or any kind of behavior that our parents continually put us down for in some way, either explicitly through verbal or physical abuse, or by subtle rejection. For example, let's say it's very unsafe to be angry around Mom. If the child displays anger and her mother is present, she is shamed and rejected. "Stop that! You can't do that, it's wrong, you're bad! If you get angry, you're a bad girl, it's not feminine." Or perhaps Mom becomes inexplicably distant, irritated and sullen, and the child thinks, "I did something bad to make Mom this way." How many of us know what that's all about?

Once this kind of interaction gets internalized, it creates a "double bind." In the case of anger, if someone provokes us and anger is actually the healthy and appropriate response, we will intuitively feel that we are justified to be angry. But because of being shamed for being angry we will deny our "true self" who is correct, and tell ourselves we are bad for feeling angry. Thus we see ourselves as bad because we feel angry, and we are bad because we want to feel angry, and we are bad because we are angry at those who have shamed us for being angry. No matter which way we turn, we are "bad." So we turn on ourselves, and shame is the result.

It is the same dynamic with sex. As a child begins to develop, there are sexual drives and manifestations of sexuality that are normal. If a child is continually shamed about it, what can happen later on, say in teenage years, whenever those sexual drives manifest themselves (which in teenage years is quite frequent—constant even), what comes out is not the sexual drive, but an experience of shame, self-blame, and self-contempt. "Oh, I'm defective. I'm having these desires I shouldn't have. Oh, I'm attracted to this person, I must be evil, I must be broken." One of the sickest things about our culture is how men treat one another, especially when it comes to the teenage years. A very typical thing in our culture is that Dad will quit giving his son a hug because it's not manly. Well, that's nonsense.

There is a very sick confusion in our culture, which we have to overcome, between touch and sexuality. Just because somebody wants to be touched, held, or hugged doesn't necessarily mean that they are approaching you in a sexual manner. The two are totally distinct things. And it doesn't mean that because your teenage son wants to get a hug from his dad that he's homosexual. It's absolutely not what it means at all. He needs the physical nurture, he needs the love, he needs the affirmation of the relationship, and he needs fundamentally to be able to identify with his dad. This is one area where young men in our culture are horribly shamed, and it's something that has created a rupture in our culture, an autonomous individualism which results in most men being profoundly withdrawn. Often, men don't know how to have a friendship with one another. It's sick. This is something fundamentally dysfunctional with our culture.

Now, this dynamic of shame can happen for any normal human affect: fear, distress, anger or enjoyment. We can be shamed for showing fear of something as well as for enjoying something that, in itself, is entirely appropriate. It's very irritating when a little child is crying and crying, and so the parent reacts and tries to hush the child, and in frustration shames the child into silence. Eventually the child learns it is unsafe to cry for any reason. So when someone is feeling distressed, instead of crying, self-contempt, self-blame come out, and they beat themselves up for feeling like crying. This happens, especially with a young child in a preverbal stage, but it can also be equally powerful with adults.

So, fundamentally, healthy relationships are an affirmation of what it means to be truly human, and to be accepted in love in spite of our human failures and shortcomings. Our children will find their true selves through identification with a loving parent who affirms them. But this is not just true for children—adults need affirmation too. On one hand, one can go to excess in building up someone's ego, but that's not what true affirmation is about. Affirmation is about saying, "You're all right. You're a real person. Yes, we all have failings, you did wrong, but you're OK. I care about you anyway." In other words, it's a relationship in which we experience unconditional love.

Question and Answer Session

Can you talk a little bit about family dynamics? I know people who are 35 years old and have never left home, and it seems like with the current economic situation and parents living longer it is getting more difficult for a child to "differentiate," or perhaps leave a dysfunctional family situation.

+Jonah: We all know people who might still be involved in the kind of relationship where we have to be a caregiver to our parents, and where there hasn't been the ability to fundamentally differentiate, so that the life of the child is completely absorbed still in the life of the parent—the 35 year old who's never left home. Now on one hand, there's some very admirable things about self-sacrifice that we have to look at and it's not necessarily dysfunction and not necessarily shame. But we have to look at what are the fundamental underlying motivations and dynamics of the family.

The fact that we see it as a "problem" that the 35 year old has not left home is part of our modern culture. A hundred years ago the 35 year old lived with his parents and maybe his grandparents. The family stuck together.

+Jonah: Right, but I'm not talking about multigenerational families. I'm talking about the person who's so dependent on their parents that they're unable to leave home.

One of the last messages I want to get across is—absolutely the last thing I would ever want to say is that multigenerational families are bad. I think they're probably the healthiest things that can possibly be, because the disintegration of the family has disintegrated our culture. And the first step of that disintegration was fifty years ago with the development of the nuclear family, as opposed to the extended family. We didn't have nuclear families up until fifty years ago. Before then, "families" weren't autonomous, self contained "dad, mom and the kids", they were multi-generational.

That's one of the things I'd like to talk about this morning, the effect of shame on the family, and how that works. This is important because now that the nuclear family has disintegrated, the family is no longer "dad, mom and kids", it is a lot of single people with kids. But more than that, the whole notion of "family" seems to be falling by the wayside in our culture of radical individualism. Forty percent or more of the adults are living singly. Now if they were monastic that would be one thing, but monastics were only one percent at the absolute most, even in the most pious cultures that have ever existed, maybe five percent in Byzantium at its height a thousand years ago. But now, 40% of adults live singly, and 60% of marriages dissolve.

We're talking about some serious issues, and all of this is profoundly related to shame and the effect of shame on the family. Part of the fundamental effect of shame is withdrawal into oneself. What shame does is distort relationships. It distorts our ability to relate with one another and have authentic intimacy, because what shame essentially does is distort our boundaries. We are created with an innate need for identification with another person. A child has to identify with his parents. In a monastery, the novices have to be able to identify with the spiritual father. In a women's monastery, the novices identify with the spiritual mother. In a family, the parents are the identification figures for the children, and the husband and the wife are identification figures for one another. This is very important. It is through relationships that we also differentiate and realize our unique personhood. Ideally, those fundamental relationships are intended by God to constitute an authentic healthy set of relationships, which constitute and realize and actualize our very personhood, who we truly are. We don't exist autonomously. We're not solitary individuals of independent origination. What is it in the Four Noble Truths of Buddhism? We're all completely inter-dependent. There's nobody who doesn't have parents. We're all inter-dependent. And the nature of that interdependency is what enables us to actualize our personhood, to attain fulfillment, to attain wholeness, to attain authentic life. Not just existence, but life. And when that is hampered by shame, then there's something essential within us that is not being fulfilled.

What are the sources of shame?

+Jonah: Abuse, abandonment, as I mentioned, being overtly or covertly shamed. Shame is something that can almost be inherited. Unhealthy shame can be passed on from generation to generation by the nature of interactions within the family. For example, one of the hardest things about family relationships is that we basically repeat the ways we have been treated. If we have been treated a certain way, we will most likely treat our children in that same way. It's all for the most part kind of unconscious. So if you had a strong domineering mother who was abusive, most likely you're going to be abusive. If in your family system there is this kind of radical perfectionism, that's going to be something that's going to get passed on from generation to generation through the expectations. (And perfectionism is something I want to go into later.)

Another aspect of shame, or the effects of shame, is addiction, whether it be to substances, consuming something like food or drugs. Some people struggle with behavioral addictions like sex, work, or exercise, or even addictions in thought, or even religious addictions. That's something we need to talk about later too, because there's a lot of very toxic religious problems. But, these tend to get passed on as patterns of behavior. So if your father was an alcoholic, very likely not only will you emerge codependent, which essentially means you have no sense of yourself, but there's a very great likelihood that you too will be alcoholic. What is an addictive behavior? It's an attempt to medicate oneself from the pain of the shame. An addiction becomes a front-level defense to try to stop the pain, because shame is something that is profoundly painful. A feeling that one is bad, or defective, or inadequate or broken, is very painful, especially when it gets constantly reinforced. Now, that's just one level.

Another level, one deeper into the self, are the ego defenses. What are the defenses we see when we're feeling shamed by someone or something? We see rage, arrogance, power and control, depression, withdrawal, envy, contempt, blame, denial, perfectionism, and shamelessness. All of these are very closely related to the passions. You think about the carnal passions, gluttony, lust, avarice (desire for things), the passions of the soul, anger, despondency, envy, and the even deeper passions of vainglory and pride. All of these are means of defending ourselves. Think about pride. Think about how hollow it is. Often we can see right through it, in others especially. We can identify pride when people are boastful and arrogant, and trying to paint a false image of themselves through their words, through their actions, through their resources. But how often do we see through that, and realize that there's a very broken and very sad person behind it. And depression—there's not a whole lot that needs to be said about depression. It also can be a profound reaction, an attempt to defend against shame. Depression, among other things, is deep withdrawal into oneself. If you're totally withdrawn, and become like a turtle, and pull in your head and your limbs all curled up, with all you present to the world being a hard shell, then it's pretty hard to get to you. It's a refusal to relate.

One issue we often don't connect with shame, is power and control. I think everyone knows what it's like to be in the presence of someone who has to control every situation. They come in and dominate the conversation. It has to be their agenda, it has to be their outlook. You can't get a word in edgewise because they are the "big" personality. Well that big personality is very often a very broken frightened person who has to control everything and every one, and is unable to allow people to be themselves, for fear of being challenged and being hurt, shamed. All of these manifestations have huge gradations and can have huge consequences. A control freak can become somebody like Hitler or Stalin, devastating others with a need for control. The last thing you want is for somebody who's a control freak, who has power and control issues that are fundamentally shame based, to be in a position of authority. It's frightening, even terrifying.

Envy. How much of envy is based on shame?

+Jonah: Envy is comparison-making. "They have that because they're better. I want that, but I'm not good enough to have it." It comes from self contempt. I want that, I want that, I want that. I can't have that. So what happens with envy is you start cutting the other person down, you become their enemy, it breaks communion, and it just turns into tragedy.

You mentioned perfectionism . . .

+Jonah: One of the biggest problems in family systems especially in certain cultural contexts, is perfectionism, where the expectations put on a child are unreasonably high. When I was a kid, the grading scale was this: A was alright, B was bad, and C is failure. In other words, "You better not come home with a C." Not that that was put on me by my parents, it was my own perfectionism coming out of me. This unhealthy kind of perfectionism is one where a person is only valued for what they do. In other words, love is conditional. "I will love you if you get an A. I will value you if you can do this well, and if you can't do this well, then I don't want to have anything to do with you. I will ignore your existence." This is something that can be very subtle. Even in its subtlety it can be profoundly damaging to oneself, because ultimately, we will end up creating God in our own damaged image of self rejection and conditional love. What we're called to, and what is healthy, is not a conditional kind of approach to acceptance of a child, or an adult, on the basis of what they can do and how well they can do it. Rather, we have to accept each other unconditionally.

We have all sorts of things to talk about in regards to religion and perfectionism. "Oh, they're not Orthodox enough." Or our shame based self-loathing, "I'm not orthodox enough." When you combine perfectionist shame with internalized shame, say from abuse or abandonment, it's going to turn into a pretty sorry situation. We need healing from this.

That constant striving for perfection—because that's the only way that I know that I am going to be accepted, that I am going to be able to have my needs fulfilled—is a defense against shame, and it's based in fear. Almost all of these are based in fear. If I don't rage against that person who's offending me, he's going to hurt me even more. If I don't completely shut myself up like an oyster, and just refuse to relate, I'm going to get very badly hurt. If I don't completely dominate everything and everyone round me, they're going to hurt me. This stuff is very primal, fight or flight.

Another way that we not only defend against shame but transfer it, is by blaming. We all know what that's like. How easy it is to try to blame somebody else and transfer that shame. You mess up and say to the other, "Why didn't you tell me I was going in the wrong direction?" There's a story used in the literature about a little kid who's helping dad with the car, and he says, "Get that wrench." There's an array of wrenches. He goes and gets one, and the father says, "You stupid idiot, why didn't you get me the right wrench?" Blame, rather than accepting responsibility for not expressing what was needed. And then there's the reaction of contempt. If there's a situation we find ourselves in, in which we feel shamed by somebody, often we hold them in contempt. We find some reason to view them condescendingly and look down on them, to disregard their existence, and react to them with disgust. I don't think that needs any example. Now, those are defenses against shame. Is it fairly clear how these are defenses and how they work?

You're going to go into the other part about how the child who gets shamed defends himself?

+Jonah: Well, basically, children often can't. This is where fear and hopelessness and powerlessness come in.

Let's take that situation into another one. What if it's a boss, and you're an employee, how does the employee protect himself from an abusive boss, one who shames people?

+Jonah: One of the greatest sources of shame among adults is a sense of powerlessness. This is especially acute where you have an employer/employee relationship. If your boss is into shaming you, you basically have no power to resist. What can you do? You just get squashed and squashed and squashed. So that can be a profoundly shaming experience. Your boss comes up to you and says, "Why did you quote that loan at a quarter point below what we can deliver? Who do you think you are? Where do you think you're going to get that money from?" And on and on and on. Well, what do you do? You just shrink down in shame, or you get angry. If you get contemptuous towards your boss you're going to get fired. If you rage, you're going to get fired. If you blame him, you're going to get fired. And so all this fear comes up. So we have that sense of powerlessness, especially in the workplace, or in a marriage, or in all sorts of situations. Or even in the church.

But then what do you do?

+Jonah: Well, what do you do? I think that's something we have to look at and understand. I don't claim in any way to have all the answers to this. Ultimately, I think we see what to do when we see what's going on, because 90% of it is trying to make conscious our unconscious reactions. If we understand that we are reacting in a certain way because we're being shamed and therefore our defenses are going up, we already have control over it. I had this wonderful spiritual father when I was in seminary, Bishop Kallistos. He had three points to his spirituality: Do not resent, do not react, and keep inner stillness. It's all about not reacting. It's what the whole spiritual life is really all about. What is resentment? Resentment is essentially shame-based, a reaction, an internal reaction. It's trying to maintain anger, contempt, disgust at somebody for having offended us, which usually means shamed us, in some way or another.

Father Jonah, in dealing with people that shame us, it can also be helpful (it's not easy) if you know that they are frightened. Then you can respond not so much to them dumping shame on you, but to their fear. It can change the dynamic.

+Jonah: Again, it's being conscious and controlling your reaction. If all you're doing is reacting, then you're not going to be mindful enough of the other person as "person," but rather objectifying him as this shaming object. And so there's this very profound dynamic that goes on between relating to people as subjects, or if we are living through our false self, as two objects: "it" and "it," rather than two persons, "I" and "Thou." One of the ways in which shame arises is the situation where we expect to be dealt with as a person in a relationship, a person who's valued, who's loved, in a context of communion, and instead we're dealt with as an object. Shame is going to arise out of that. It's going to be a shaming event.

So what would a normal correction of a child be like then as they get angry? How would you correct them?

+Jonah: I think probably you pick them up and hold them. You pull them out of the situation, which stops the behavior and reinforces your acceptance of them as a person, and that you love them, even though they're angry, and that it's OK to be angry. This is very important. It is OK to be angry. You know the Scriptures say, "Be angry, and do not sin" (Eph. 4:26). Now for most of us, it's very hard to be angry and not sin, because how does our anger, which is usually a shame-based rage, express itself? "I want to lash out, I want to punch the person. I want to contemptuously degrade them." It becomes irrational. So the whole task is to take this and make it a rational process, not just to react emotionally, but to bring yourself under control. So instead of reacting passionately, you can respond rationally.

Talk about religious addiction.

+Jonah: If I'm a perfectionist and acting "righteous, righteous, righteous" and thinking myself really good and holy (compared to other people) because I'm keeping all the rules and canons, or if I see myself as "righteous" because "Jesus has taken all my sins," then I'm not going to be able to see the pain inside myself, I'm not going to look for its roots, or at it, I'm going to live in denial. I'm not going to be able to feel the pain inside because I'm focusing all of my attention and effort and thoughts on this attempt to create an image. In other words, it's called an idealized self. To live according to an idealized image of oneself means not living in reality. It's delusion, or *prelest*.

And so this is a big thing in religion, whether it's "righteous, righteous, righteous," or I'm going to be the perfect Greek monk, or the perfect Russian monk. Or I'm going to be the perfect "Orthodox Christian" because I'm going to wear all the right clothes, and do all the right things, go to all the services, and know all the right words. Well, personally, I can't be the perfect Russian monk. First of all, I'm not Russian. I know the language, but I don't know the culture. It's not who I am. It's not real. What all this shame-based stuff in our personality does is create insecurity. We're insecure in our identity, we don't know who we really are, so we put on a "self" by engaging in externals. This is one of the big things for Orthodox converts. We think, "If I just get everything right." If I say all the right prayers, and do everything just right, and it looks just right, whether its Russian peasant look of the 17th century, or whether its Greek monastic look of the 18th century, or whether its Greek archdiocese look of the 21st century, with just the right haircut and just the right $800 suit you go to church in or the clerical garb you'd mortgage your soul for, or anything in between those. A lot of that is based in our insecurity. We aren't simply being who we are: Americans in the 21st century, in northern California, who believe in Christ. And that's what it is. That's what being an Orthodox Christian is. It's not about all the other stuff. It's not about all the other stuff AT ALL. The more we delude ourselves into this external formalism, the farther we're going to get from an authentic relationship with Christ, because we're going to be so preoccupied about external forms that we lose the content.

There's a great story about this monk who came to visit the Orthodox Institute in Paris. It was a Russian émigré thing, so all the classes were conducted in Russian. So the monk got up and was giving this talk about Russian monasticism. And the bishop was sitting there who was the main professor of the course. The visiting monk talked about what they did in the monastery, the rule and the order of things, and especially how they dressed and what it means and what they ate and all the rules, and you can eat this during lent and not this, and you can have canola oil but not olive oil, because who's ever seen what a canola looks like anyway . . . the holy fathers never saw a canola to begin with. And the bishop at the end of the talk said, in Russian, "You talked about how you dressed yourself and what you ate, but not how you worked out your salvation." And what's important? It's working out your salvation. None of the rest of this stuff matters. It has no eternal significance whatsoever. It can drag you into hell though. That's an eternal consequence, because we can create idols out of externals. Something occurred to me this morning, that our egoism is idolatry, because, really, when we become so wrapped up in this false identity that we create, that's what it is, it's egoism. That's how the holy fathers in the contemporary translation put it . . . ego-ism. And it's idolatry. The exaltation of our ego-created "objective self" . . . It's idolatry. How easily we fall into idolatry. How did St John end his epistle? "Little children, keep yourselves from idols."

I wonder if you'd like to comment on some idolatry a little closer to home for North Americans. Busy-ness and work-aholism are what I understand to be predominant defenses against shame in our culture. I wonder if you wanted to open that up.

+Jonah: Sure. You know we keep ourselves so busy and so distracted. I mean, how many houses do you go into where there's not a TV going, constantly, or a radio going, constantly? In our culture, every-where we walk in, everyplace you go has music playing. It has some-thing going on, it has sound, it has advertising. It has this utter bombardment of images, all of which are ads for the passions. You look at some half-naked woman on the side of the bus—or half-naked man in San Francisco—advertising I don't know what. That's what sells in San Francisco. In our culture we are constantly bombarded with images. What is that doing to our psyche? It is distracting us from looking at ourselves.

Work-aholism is especially an issue in our culture. But it's just like any other kind of addiction. It's being addicted to work, and so we're so busy that we don't have time to realize that maybe I'm a mess, and I need to get some help. "I don't want to deal with that. I don't want to deal with my problems. I'm just going to work." Then there's per-fectionism tied in with it. "Oh, I have to have that big new house and it has to be in just the right location, and in just the right school dis-trict." Isn't this the classic American dream? "I have to have this, I have to have that," aren't we consumed by consumerism? And, "I am not a good American, I'm not a good person unless I have such and such toys." The new Mercedes, the new BMW, the big new house, the right computer. This is idolatry, and we define ourselves by these things, and not only by having them, but also by the ability to possess them and the ability to possess them comes out of our work. What is that work ethic based in? It's probably based in the fear of being judged as a lazy good-for-nothing. It's based in fear. Who needs all the stuff that we get? It's all a wonderful distraction from dealing with ourselves.

I have a story. There's a monk who's sitting outside a cave and he was mumbling to himself and crying—and someone came by and said, "What's the problem?" and he said "Here I've been on Mt Athos (or wherever it was) for 30 years trying to attain perfect prayer, and I haven't attained it." And the elder who'd come by scratched his head and said, "You missed the point." I think the whole area of our spirituality is sort of like we can do all this stuff in the name of being spiritual, and I think one of the most dangerous vices in this area is vainglory. In the spiritual life, we get tripped up by it all the time, and it's very subtle.

+Jonah: Let's talk about toxic religion a little bit more. If we are "religious" we have to look at our motivations. We talked about this false righteousness and the false "religious self" of ego idolatry. In Orthodoxy, we all appreciate beautiful liturgy and practice of prayer, and for the most part it's very stable and not focused on creating an "exciting worship experience." But even in the liturgy, or through practices of prayer or meditation, or contemplation, we can experience changes in our moods and emotions. One of the things that we can do is confuse that mood alteration with an "experience of grace," and make these things ends in themselves, so that we're going to church in order to feel good instead of to worship God for His sake. We go to get distracted from our problems. How often, especially if we have some kind of perfectionist shame within us, do we also not fall into judging and criticizing others, of looking at how others are living their religious lives, and then comparing ourselves to them for validation of the self-idol we've created.

Calvinism creates an image of God that's a punitive arbitrary Deity whose nature it is to cast us depraved people into the burning fiery abyss. There's a reason for perfectionism right there. But that's certainly not the God of Jesus Christ. Then there's the idea that the human person is absolutely unable to do anything good. Now, it is true, the whole idea of synergy is that we enter into God's action, and our good actions are done in communion with God and in synergy with God, not "on our own power." But there's a Calvinist twist on that which leads to despair. It's the idea that I am garbage, I am worthless, that anything I do is only by God's sovereign arbitrary grace, because I am totally unable to do anything unless God arbitrarily chooses me and gives me the power. What it leads to is paralysis. "I'm unable to perceive the will of God, so I'm just going to sit and wait until I get hit over the head with a 2 x 4 by God, who's going to show me what to do." What is most important for us to understand about God is His love for us. His love is absolutely unconditional—we don't have to do anything for God to love us.

What is repentance? Repentance is not about beating ourselves up because we've slipped and fallen in a certain way. Repentance is about reordering—*metánoia*—the transformation of the mind, the turning of the mind to God. It is turning the *nous* to God, away from its attention scattered throughout our various passions, including feeling sorry for ourselves because we've been shamed. It is the transformation of the mind, the redirection of the mind back to God. Yes, it's important to feel sorry that we've sinned, that is healthy shame. But to become completely possessed by our own self-pity is not what repentance is about. Self-pity is a very important thing to think about, because how often do we fall into self-pity? Instead of simply admitting our mistake and going on, we stay in the shame. St John Climacus talks about it. One of the fundamental tasks is that when we fall, we get up again. I like to see the prostrations that we do during Lent as an image of our falling and getting up again. It's only the demons whose nature it is to not get up again when they fall. But often what we do when we fall is wallow in our own self-pity, and that doesn't help. It doesn't help at all. We need to simply pick ourselves up again, brush ourselves off and keep going. Go to confession, and keep going.

Sometimes, I feel I'm expected to conform to an "image" of what an "Orthodox Christian should" be or look like or not look like. When

I come into church, I should get rid of my makeup, not be a southern California housewife, wear long dresses, and so on.

+Jonah: There are people who are trying to shame other people into conforming to their own "religious self images," though perhaps not consciously. Some reject all forms and externals because of their own fear and their own negative experiences of the church and religion. But it is just the flip side of the coin to be legalistic about others' appearances. Wearing a Hawaiian shirt or a black turtle neck to Church can both be "statements" or manifestations of a false self. These reactions all come from someplace, and it is not from union with God. So I think part of it is first, not to allow ourselves to react in a judgmental way against them, but rather to look at their fear and their feelings.

Second, we really need to ask, what does it mean to be an Orthodox Christian? What does that mean for my life, what does that mean for my lifestyle? If it's something that comes from your heart to put on a long dress and not wear makeup and not go to the beautician, that can be a very profound act of piety, and something deep and authentic. But if it's just a matter of trying to uphold some external standard, and about somebody else's opinions of you and avoiding rejection and shame, and if it is not coming from your own heart, then you really need to question what you are doing. You need to ask yourself, "What am I trying to express? What would happen to my self image if I didn't do this?" Ultimately, we need to look at our own motivations. "Am I trying to be something that I'm not? Am I trying to appear to look like something I'm not? Am I a southern California housewife trying to look like a nun?" You have to look at that. On the other hand, am I going to flaunt being a southern California housewife, and go to church in shorts and a halter top? So we have to look at our inner motivations, and be real with ourselves.

We need to ask, "Who am I and what does it mean for me to be in this particular community where I live and worship?" Say, you go into a typical established Antiochian parish in southern California with your headcovering, long skirt, long sleeved turtleneck shirt and 2 sweaters, and it's 90 degrees outside. You have 300 knot prayer ropes dragging the floor, and 3 crosses, and all the other women are sitting there dressed like normal Americans. Something's not right. Aside from looking weird and looking like you are trying to draw attention to yourself, there may be lots of other things going on underneath that.

So the question is, what is humility? There's no humility in that. It becomes something that draws attention to oneself; it becomes something that is coming out of vainglory. It'd be just like going into a community where the norm for the women is to wear long skirts, and to be dressed in shorts and a halter-top. The point would be to draw attention to oneself, or to make a statement about the others, out of pride and vainglory. Those are cover-ups for insecurity and desire for attention, and wanting to be accepted or being judgmental or controlling. Most likely one would be looking for exactly the wrong kind of acceptance, because of some kind of abuse and shame in the past.

How we dress can be a very important thing, because it can reveal a lot. One of the things about monasteries is that you don't have to worry about what your clothes are. It's a uniform and that's it. It's just a uniform. In the world, we use clothes as a means of self-expression. But what is that self-expression? What is the self, which is that false identity, that identity we've constructed, and what is that false self expressing?

We all know the image of the young zealous convert. Some kid gets all fired up. A new convert, he goes off to a monastery for a visit. He's got prayer ropes all up and down both arms, a great big cross out in front of his shirt, he's making his sign of the cross in a grandiose manner, and saying to everyone around him, "You're not really Orthodox." You can see right through it; it's totally transparent. He's trying to be something he's not. He's not there. So it's a matter of really looking at how the passions work. Now I'm not suggesting that we should all sit and psychoanalyze the person who goes and does this, because that's a typical thing for a young kid to do. There's vainglory, all sorts of vainglory, working in there. There's pride and self-opinion, and perfectionism. "I have to be totally conformed to the external form, otherwise I'm not going to be really Orthodox." It's that kind of false righteousness that results in judgmentalism and criticism, and then the inevitable, "Well, my jurisdiction is better than your jurisdiction" kind of thing. Or, "Your jurisdiction is better than mine and I better go join your jurisdiction because mine is run by a bunch of creeps." (However he defines creeps.) All this stuff is just distraction from the one thing that is needful, which is the focus on Jesus Christ, the focus on entering into and maintaining communion with God, and dealing with our own issues so that we can be purified and healed of vainglory.

Vainglory is one of the sneakiest of the passions. St John Climacus writes about it a lot in the *Ladder*. But he talks about how some passions may heal others. He talks about how if you come upon some people who are gossiping and slandering somebody, that it's better to be seasoned with vainglory and say, "Please, brother, stop, this is not appropriate." It's better to be a little vainglorious, than to fall into slander and gossip.

That's why when you see the saints, many times they have something that happens, and they tell the people around who observe this, "Don't tell anyone about this until after I'm dead," because of the vainglory and the pride. But it looks like what I'm hearing is that we have to watch every move we make.

+Jonah: Well, in a sense we do, and that's part of it. We have to be watchful. The actual title of the *Philokalia* is *Writings of the Holy Neptic Fathers*, those who are watchful. But what is that watchfulness? We can be completely obsessed about watching our own behavior, but how much of that is really about egocentrism and vainglory, so that we can be truly righteous in the sight of men? The true watchfulness that we're called to, is to maintain our vision of God, to maintain our conscious communion with God. If we maintain that conscious communion with God, if our focus is entirely on God, if we're wrapped in the love of God, then everything else works out. If you're wrapped in the love of God, you're probably not going to be slandering your neighbor, you're probably not going to rage against somebody who just offended you. You're probably going to be just like Jesus and just accept it. What the Holy Fathers tell us is that one of the goals of the spiritual life is dispassion, or *apáthia*. Not apathy as we understand it, but *apáthia*, dispassion, which means to be unmoved. So that somebody can rage against you, can insult you, can even murder you, like people did to Jesus, and you can remain unmoved. He didn't withdraw in shame, He didn't rage back, He didn't regard them with contempt and curse them. What did He say? "Father, forgive them for they don't know what they're doing. Into Your hands I commend My spirit." It's acceptance.

CHAPTER 7

Shame and Humility

(Adapted from Audio Transcript of a Retreat in Inverness, CA)

It is important and valuable to consider the relationship between shame and humility. One thing I've observed is that we confuse the two. How often do we have this image of humility as being a cringing, cowering doormat? We think this is some kind of an ideal to strive for. A corollary is to confuse repentance with being ridden with guilt, and watchfulness as being constant self-psychoanalysis. All of these things are related.

What effect does shame have on us? It encourages us to withdraw from relationships. We become totally enclosed within ourselves. When we're feeling shamed, or harbor deep internalized shame and are living in reaction to it, and let it define our character, we cut ourselves off from everyone and everything through all these defenses in order to try to avoid being hurt any further. We're like wounded animals trying to protect ourselves. But this is exactly not humility, and it's certainly nothing that is desirable.

Another aspect of a false view of humility and shame is humiliation. Unfortunately, there are some practices, especially within the church both in regards to the hierarchy and the clergy, where some think that they need to bring people to "humility" through shaming and humiliation. But the result is not humility, it is submission through abuse. It is the same as dysfunctional parents dealing with their children. They think that by shaming them and humiliating them they're going to be able to get the child to comply, or do better, or stop a certain behavior.

What then is true humility? Authentic humility is a profound openness. It's transparency with God and with other people. It's a state of being very spiritually mature and secure. In authentic humility, nothing will be able to ruffle you. Nothing will be able to disturb your basic peace, because that peace is rooted in your relationship with God, and in that living conscious experience of God which permeates every aspect of life.

From that perspective, there's no fear of what anyone or anything can do to you. As St John says, "There is no fear in love, but perfect love casts out fear" (I Jn. 4:18). Rather, everything can be accepted as a gift of God's providence, both the bitter as well as the sweet, both the praise and the adulation, as well as the abuse. We see in our Lord Jesus Christ the ultimate example of what authentic humility is. Nothing, nothing could disturb that bond of communion. Nothing could shatter that love. Nothing could destroy that sense of Jesus' being loved by God, no matter what people did and said to Him, even when they murdered Him.

We see this image in Christ of authentic humility, but not in a sense of being weak. In reality, this is the complete and absolute opposite of weakness. In the terms of the world, perhaps it might be considered weakness not to fight back. But we would say that the values and the approach of the world and the understanding of the world is something that is utterly sick and unhealthy. The authentic way, the most healthy way—the way in which we actualize and realize our true personhood—is by attaining to that most sublime and perfect humility.

Now, it's also important to look at the role of guilt in this. When we are in the middle of Lent, listening to the hymns of the Lenten Triodion, we hear them go on and on and on about realizing our sins and how far we've fallen. If we have a healthy self-esteem and a sense of that connection with God in authentic humility, being rooted in the sense that God's love is absolutely unconditional, then we can accept what is being said. "I am the greatest of sinners, I have sinned immeasurably, my sins are greater than the number of the sands of the sea," and so forth. This can be a productive kind of shame and guilt which moves us to repentence.

However, if we're approaching it from a shame-based perspective, then instead of hearing that "I can repent and God's love remains unconditional for me and he will accept my repentance," we hear, "I am bad, I am evil, I am hopeless, I am damned, and I have nothing left but to despair." If we beat ourselves up with our sins, if we allow ourselves to fall into self-blame and self-contempt, we are reading the ascetical literature wrongly. I would submit to you that is exactly the opposite of what the writers of that hymnography and ascetical literature intended. But from a shame-based perspective, that's very often the reaction that people have when exposed to the ascetical literature. "I am bad, I am broken, I have no hope of salvation, I might as well give up and kill myself."

We have to look and see how we are understanding this. Are we grasping it with the right frame of mind? Where does all this hymnography lead us? If it is leading us into despair, it is a misunderstanding. If we are led into hopelessness and guilt, what that points to is that we have issues within ourselves. We are too ashamed, and we have a dysfunctional shame and guilt reaction when we feel or hear ourselves accused by someone else, or even by the services, or by the prayers, or by the literature of the church. The problem is not the literature of the Church, it is that we have a shame reaction which underlies our own feeling of worthlessness.

Part of my guess is that the great Byzantine Fathers who wrote this material, both the ascetical literature and the hymnography, were from the highest levels of the aristocracy. They were superbly educated. In other words, they were spoiled, rich Greek kids. And there's probably not a whole lot of difference between spoiled, rich Greek kids now and the ones of a thousand years ago. What is the family in that culture like? Think about it. It's a family structure that is exuberantly effusive and supportive. These children probably had no abandonment issues. If you read between the lines of the literature, the problem was exactly the opposite of self-hatred—it was pride. It was this totally over-inflated self-opinion, which is what you would probably get from an upbringing in which a kid from the upper levels of the aristocracy is spoiled to death. That's who wrote the material, the hymnography, and most of the ascetical literature. Now they repented from pursuing a life of the world, and most of them entered the monastic life and became great ascetics. So they realized that their egos were totally over-inflated. That is really the primary, underlying passion that is dealt with in most of the ascetic literature.

One of the things that I asked several scholars such as Deacon John Chryssavgis from Holy Cross, Fr Tom Hopko, as well as several spiritual fathers both here as well as in Russia and Greece, was this: Where in the Holy Fathers do they deal with self-hatred and self-blame, to the point where it becomes toxic? Their answers? They didn't know of a place where the Holy Fathers dealt with it. It's certainly not in the literature available in English, which is very small in proportion to what is actually in the original languages.

Now there are glimmers of it in certain places, but I think the depth and pervasiveness of this is the result of the disintegration of the extended family and the disintegration of society in the West following the Second World War, and now the disintegration of the nuclear family at the end of the Cold War. Our culture has descended into autonomous individualism, which is completely and totally defenseless against massive internalized shame. Abandonment is one of the central issues that laid the groundwork for internalized shame and for self-hatred.

Abandonment issues don't just occur because someone was dropped off at an orphanage and forgotten. An infant being dropped off at day care and forgotten for 5 days out of the week can feel tremendously abandoned. One of the most central issues of the nurturing of children is that essential bond between the mother and the child that happens during breast feeding. It is that physical touch, but also the eye contact, that bonding that comes with the mother gazing with love and joy and care into the eyes of her child while he or she is nursing. I believe it is not just coincidence that the family began disintegrating and that bottles came after the Second World War. In spite of all of human history, it is now considered socially inappropriate to be nursing a child that is more than 8 months old. Nonsense. I have one friend who nursed her children until they were almost four years old (or at least it was available). We have to think, "What is the impact of the popular culture on me, and what is it doing to my family? What is my motivation?" If a woman wants to be a mother, but also wants to have her own career and pursue her own "personal fulfillment" at the expense of her children, what she is going to do is create lots of work for therapists twenty or thirty years later. Now that's great for the psychoanalytic profession, but what it does is create a whole bunch of messed-up kids.

The real effect of the experience of emotional abandonment—even if it's completely unintentional on the part of the parent or parents—is that it creates this sense in the child that "I am not worth the attention of this person who is the most important to me, that my life depends on. Therefore my life isn't worth anything." It lays the groundwork for self-hatred. It lays the groundwork for the feeling of worthlessness and despair. It fundamentally disrupts the ability to create relationships. That bonding in the earliest years of the child's life with its mother is the basis and foundation of relationships for the rest of life. What that does is lay the basic foundation for trust. A lot of the stuff in dealing with these issues is very, very primal and basic. You're talking about fear, about trust. An infant thinks: Will Mom will come back when I cry? When I'm hungry? Am I'm going to be fed? That's a large part of what an infant is dealing with. It's these essential and basic kinds of emotions and issues that lay the basic foundation for how we deal with everything and everyone later on in our life. Will we have enough trust to form a lasting relationship with anyone? Can we open ourselves to anyone? What this is laying is the groundwork for the opportunity for intimacy.

So what is intimacy? It's the dropping of barriers, the dropping of our boundaries. Now, we always have to have certain boundaries. Part of psychological health is to have appropriate, intact boundaries. But it's also to know when to open yourself to another, and to be able to authentically and truly expose yourself without fear, fear of shame, without fear of being ridiculed. This goes back to humility: One of the most fundamental elements about humility is that there is no fear in humility. What can anyone do to you? If you're with God, no one can do anything to you. They can kill the body, but so what? This is the humility of the martyrs. This is the faith of the martyrs.

As we look at the whole foundation of our being able to relate to others, this foundational nurture is the beginning of our objective self-awareness. The infant who is being held and cared for and treasured is forming his self image, his awareness of his person in relationship to his mother. His proper formation will always be at the sacrificial expense of the mother. That's just part of what being a mother is about. One thing that I really believe is that the greatest ascetics are young mothers. They are far more ascetical than any monk going off and doing his own will. A monk (or anyone) can choose not to fast. You can choose to break the fast, you can choose to break your spiritual disciplines. But a mother can't choose not to feed that child. Right? She can't choose. Well, she can choose, but then she's going to be murdering the child. So, really, she can't choose to do that.

Motherhood is an image and real foundation of what authentic self-denial is. As a new mother, you're not getting much back emotionally from the child in the beginning. Little children don't have a whole lot to give emotionally. That's not what they're there for. You have to be available to them, not them to you. So if you look at how their personhood is being nurtured, how the objective self-image of that child is being brought into existence, it is going to be formed differently if the basis and foundation of that is, "I can trust, I am loved unconditionally, I'm not rejected, I'm not abandoned," or, conversely, if the child never knows if Momma is going to be there. "Am I going to be crying for hours and hours and no one is going to listen to me, am I going to be rejected, am I going to be abandoned?" This constant, horrific fear lays the foundation of shame.

There's another influence in our culture which makes it even more of an impossible situation. This is the influence of the "work ethic" of Puritanism where your work proves your worth, which became a particularly American religious ideal, and still pervades the American ethos. Along with that there was the self-reliant "pioneer spirit," because the early settlers of the country were dealing with conquering the wilderness to establish a life here. So now we have this whole set of values that requires that you be about hard work, self-reliance and independence. So if you need someone, then you feel shamed about having to need someone because everything in our American history says you don't need anybody, you can do it yourself. If you need somebody, there's something wrong with you. That goes hand in hand with the other, more specific kind of shaming, and there's no way you can win. Because if you need someone and express that, then you feel shame that you even have to need someone. So I think it's very important to be critical of our culture, which is very sick.

So fundamentally, the family is the key. The family is the absolute most important element in our society which needs to be restored at all costs, not only the restoration of the nuclear family, but also the restoration of the extended family. I don't know if it strikes you as something hideous to send off our grandparents to live in ghettos of the aged. What are we doing, really? We are rejecting them. "Oh, I'd rather go out and make money than care for Mom and her illness." We have to look at our self-centeredness. We have to look at our egotism. We have to look at all these elements in which we have become obsessed with ourselves, obsessed with success in worldly terms. St Paul tells us that if we cannot take care of our own families, how can we call ourselves Christians? We are worse than an unbeliever if we do not take care of our own families (1 Tim 5:8). We have to take this to heart, and we have to critique our culture. Sometimes we even have to reject the culture and say, "No, this is not good, this is not moral, it's not healthy, and these values we're being taught are terribly wrong."

Now the real task for building an Orthodox Christian community is not about simply building a community centered around the liturgical life of the church. It's about building a community that's focused on the Gospel and caring for one another. That's real Christianity and all the formal externals and structures are secondary. It's much more important to care for your sick parents or your sick child than it is for you to go to church. I say that as a priest. If you have somebody who's totally dependent on you and you can't leave them alone, it would be a far greater sin for you to go to church than to miss church to care for that person. We build up all these perfectionist systems and form all these ideas that sound nice and pious because of all this perfectionist shame. We may have all the forms of the religion, but as St Paul says, if we have the form but deny the power (2 Tim 3:5), then what are we doing? Our life as Christians is about entering into that living experience of communion with God and with one another.

So for example, if you have a sick child or a sick parent that you need to care for, that's already a meaningful act of communion, an act of self-denial, an act of love. And God is entirely present by that act of sacrificial love, because the real task of our spiritual life, the real task of being Christian, is to live according to that communion. This is communion with God and the remembrance of God in the constant awareness of His presence through love, which of course we have to celebrate liturgically. We need to have the spiritual discipline of the communal life of the Church, we need to have the liturgical services. But our communion with one another and our communion with our neighbor is one of the most fundamental acts of what it means to be a Christian. In order to achieve that sense of relationship, we need to free ourselves from being bound by shame, it is then that we can go out and freely love our neighbor in God. Maybe our neighbor is someone who hates our guts. Maybe our neighbor is someone who does everything he can to try to shame us. What is love of the neighbor in that case? We need to ask ourselves that hard question.

Now, the way to heal the shame, according to Gershen Kaufman's language, is to restore the inter-personal bridge. The real cause of shame ultimately is the severing of personal relationship and living on the level of inter-subjectional relationship. It's the breaking of the relationship of love between an "I" and a "thou," and turning it into an "I" and an "it," whereby relationships cannot be had with people as "persons" but people are related to as objects. In order to heal this broken inter-personal bridge, we have to have and develop an authentic relationship of deep intimacy in which we can be profoundly open.

This is called a therapeutic, or healing relationship, both in the psychological and spiritual literature. You can have a therapeutic relationship with someone other than a psychotherapist. You can have a therapeutic relationship with your priest, with your spiritual father or mother, and you can have a therapeutic relationship with your husband or wife, or with your best friend. This relationship becomes the context for a deep amount of the healing of shame. It is in this kind of relationship that you learn what it means is to be authentically and completely open, and to be able to reveal the hurt, to be able to reveal the shame, without fear. Here you will be able to go back and relate the stories of those original, primal shaming scenes, and to deal with them in a way that overcomes the shame. It is rewriting those scripts and saying, "Yes, my mother shamed me as a child, and she did it in this way and that way. But now that those things are conscious, I no longer need to act according to that."

For example, if you were shamed for becoming angry, the point would be to go back, look at those situations, look at those events of shaming, and then look at it in the present and say, "I don't have to react like that. I don't need to react to the shame." You learn that, ultimately, nobody can harm you now, we can only shame ourselves. It is we who retreat into shame, or react with shame. In other words, we have control, and we don't need to simply react unconsciously and irrationally. Nobody can shame you. So we need to look and see how we have reacted in the past, and then understand how we should react now, consciously and rationally. What is a better way to react and to respond? What is a healthier way?

Now, this also comes back to humility. You may think, "If I stand up for myself and refuse to be shamed, is that something that is not an act of humility? Is that some kind of pride or egotism?" No, it's not pride or egotism. Rather, it's something that is healthy. It is healthy boundaries, and ultimately the strength of true humility in God to say, "No, I refuse to let you shame me" (you don't literally say this to the other person), or, "I refuse to let myself feel shamed in this situation."

We need to learn that if somebody is criticizing us, that doesn't mean they hate us, necessarily. Sometimes, especially with a shame-based personality, if somebody criticizes us, we think that automatically means that that person hates us and that they reject us. So what do we do in response? We reject them and close off to them as a reaction, and withdraw into our own cocoon of shame. Instead, if somebody criticizes us, what is the authentic and healthy thing to do? Part of it might be to say, "Yes, you're right. Thank you. Forgive me." The Holy Fathers say that if you are living in a monastery, there's only two words you need to learn, "bless" and "forgive." So if somebody criticizes them, they say, "Forgive me." Now, there's a lot more to it, but what is critically important is the context of unconditional love, acceptance and an "I-thou" relationship with all who live with them. You can learn to say this appropriately through being in a relationship whether it be with a spouse, whether it be with a close friend, whether it be with a spiritual mother or father, which gives us the fundamental security to know that we are unconditionally loved and unconditionally accepted.

It is important to understand that this healing and authentic humility comes only through relationship. Recently I was in contact with a person who wants to be a hermit. He feels completely rejected in life, and thinks it is better just to withdraw. One of the things that the Holy Fathers say is that nobody is given a blessing to withdraw into eremitical life, into solitude, until they are already profoundly spiritually mature. They first have to deal with all these kinds of interpersonal issues, and already be rooted in the vision of God and the living experience of communion with God, in the love of God, and the unconditionality of God's love. I'm just putting modern words to it. But if you withdraw into solitude and still have all these unresolved issues, you're going to drive yourself crazy. I think that's one of the reasons why the history of the church is littered with thousands of failed solitaries who've driven themselves nuts, either falling into delusion, or despair, or something like that.

The basic context of relationship is something absolutely fundamental in growing to an adequate spiritual maturity, and without that spiritual maturity one cannot handle solitude. Solitude is not an escape from relationships but has to flow out of true humility, a foundation of love for God and neighbor. The authentically spiritual solitary is one who has withdrawn not because he hates people or believes people hate him, but rather is in communion with everyone. It's radically different. It is not somebody who is afraid of communion with people, but rather one whose love overflows. The context for that authentic spiritual formation, whether it is in a monastery, or whether it be for lay people in a parish, is a strong and healthy network of relationships of authentic intimacy.

In the world first and foremost, this is worked out in marriage. Sixty percent of marriages fail, and I would imagine there's another large percent of those that do not fail, but where there's a profound lack of intimacy, of openness, of authentic relationship. How many have I encountered like that? There's no fulfillment. There may be sex, but that's not intimacy. We make this very wrong assumption that sex is intimacy, and it isn't so. Intimacy is an authentic openness to one another. It is honesty, love and respect. In this context, it becomes a deeply healing thing, because you can expose your wounds, and be accepted anyway. That's where the healing comes.

Ultimately this whole topic of shame leads us to the need for healing the shame. There has to be that authentic, concrete, living interpersonal relationship in order to heal. You can't do it by telephone and not by email. You can't look into someone's eyes through a television camera. You can't hold somebody and touch them and hug them and console them and give them the necessary, personal affirmation that they really are OK by email or text message. It doesn't work. It has to be a relationship of authentic intimacy, of authentic touch, of face to face incarnate communion.

Along with that there also has to be a deep striving for prayer, and not just the more surface levels of prayer, the oral prayer of reciting prayer book prayers and going to the services. That's necessary, and valuable. But I believe one of the most fundamental aspects that is needed for deep healing to authentic spiritual maturity, and deep growth to authentic spiritual maturity, is an entrance into silent prayer of the heart—the prayer of stillness, the prayer of contemplation, authentic noetic prayer. In other words, one must enter into a continual conscious awareness of God and place oneself consciously in the presence of God, standing in the presence of God in noetic awareness.

This is another difficult task. This is not the practice of the Jesus Prayer. This is beyond the Jesus Prayer. The Jesus Prayer, even though it goes into the heart, still remains words. The words themselves need to be transcended. To enter not simply into our own prayer to Jesus, but to enter into Jesus' own prayer to the Father by the Holy Spirit, so that we become consciously aware of the Holy Spirit praying within us. This is the real aim of prayer. Incidentally, the *Philokalia* is not about the Jesus Prayer. The *Philokalia* is about the prayer of inner watchfulness and stillness. It's only some of the writers of the last volume of the Philokalia that are writing about the Jesus Prayer, per se. Deep prayer, the authentic prayer of contemplation, is a prayer that is beyond words, and it's entering into that communion of love which exists between the Father and the Son in whom we have been engrafted by the Holy Spirit. It's the actualization and the realization of who we are as Christians. It is a conciousness that we have died to ourselves, and our lives are hidden with Christ in God, as St Paul says (Col 3:3).

That union in which we are united in Christ is the fulfillment of the Lord's own prayer, "That they may be one as we are one: I in them and they in me, that they may be perfectly one, that the world may know that you have sent me" (Jn. 17:21). This is that process of growth. This process of maturity, this process of spiritual life that we enter into, is this process of most profound healing. It is a healing not simply of our bodies, but of also our soul and our spirit. It is a re-formation of our identity. It's crucifying the old man, and it is a crucifixion and a resurrection in Christ, in a whole new identity, where our true identity is hidden with Christ in God. In order to be able to enter into that, we need to heal the layers of shame. In order to do that, we need this context of authentic communion in the church, a relationship with a spiritual father or a spiritual mother, and at least one other person, a close friend or one's spouse. It's that relationship that will heal us because shame is about broken relationships. Its cure is the restoration of relationship, and it is only in communion that we authentically realize and actualize the true nature of our noetic self, as an authentic person. This is our goal as human beings, to live in wholeness and in communion with God, in harmony and in synergy with His energy and activity.

Question and Answer Session

When you're talking about, you must die yourself, Fr Tom Hopko says you must die before you die. When you are the false self and that is all you know, then you realize you must "die" to that self, it does feel like a real death. Since you have a shame-based false self, the big problem is once you dismantle it, the fear is that if it is gone, there's nothing left.

+Jonah: That's why the fundamental work of dismantling can only be done in a very strong supportive and intimate relationship.

You said the hymns of Lent sound like self-hatred, but that they are really like the false self calling out, to be loved, or some aspects of ourselves to be brought in and loved, that we have rejected. But aren't there aspects of ourselves that we're trying to get rid of that we do dislike or hate?

+Jonah: You know, one of the defenses that we often use is that we split off parts of ourselves to one degree or another. Sometimes it's a pretty radical split. For example, some people who've suffered profound abuse actually split off an entire personality—and then there's the process of reintegration—because it's too shameful to face that abuse. So that whole section of personality splits away. Sometimes the more radical the abuse, the more personalities split, and this is where you get multiple personalities.

That is an extreme, but in general for most of us, we're talking about the old man and the new man. They're kind of warring with each other . . .

+Jonah: Right, but the process of healing is still fundamentally the same, and so that new man, that new person who is being resurrected and reconstructed and built in the image of Christ, is partly a whole new set of scripts, a whole new set of relationships and whole new set of senses. These are rebuilt in the context of an intimate relationship with somebody that you can identity with, and who permits that identification, and who is open to you and open to that rebuilding. So there's a whole lot of work in dismantling, and it can't happen all at once, it is not how we are "built," and it is not how we are "rebuilt." Just like learning everything that made us what we are, unlearning and relearning to become something new, it's all a slow process. You know, we as Americans want a quick solution to everything, and it doesn't happen. Sometimes it takes yeas and years and years, depending on the degree to which we've been hurt, and depending on the context in which we find ourselves. We need to find that authentic relationship with someone, with a deep sense of trust. Depending on the person and the issues, it can (or should) be done with a therapist.

For some it can be done in a monastery. In both cases it's re-parenting, in reality. And it doesn't mean that you've necessarily had horrible parents that you need to hate for the rest of your life. That's not what it is. But part of that process is to come to forgive your parents for what they were not able to give you. Then you get it, then you receive that in the context of this new relationship and start rebuilding from there. That begins that task of rebuilding. I don't know if that answers your question or not.

You were talking about the abandonment of the mother, but what about the absence of the father in the relationship. Would that tend to cause a confusion in the integration of sexual identity, if you don't have both sexes present and see a real relationship happening and have contact with both parents? They've shown that it's important for the son to have contact with the father, and the daughter to have contact with the mother, and vice versa.

+Jonah: Yes, because they're both identification images. The boy's self-acceptance as a man, often in reality, depends on his relationship with his father. A girl's self-acceptance as a woman depends on her relationship with her mother. But there's also a kind of mirroring that goes on, a type of relationship that goes on as the parent accepts the emerging sexuality of their child. How a mother relates to the emerging man in her son and how a father relates to the emerging woman in his daughter can be a tremendous point of shaming, whether it's a shaming through sexual abuse and taking advantage of them, which is a horrific problem, or whether it's some kind of subtle emotional rejection of their maturing and differentiation. I think it's a critically important thing to have both parents present.

Another thing that I think is absolutely critically important for a family is to have dinner together every night with no television. No television. Shoot it. Push it out the window, whatever. No television. Sit together and talk. One of the things I'm most profoundly grateful for in my family is that we did that. We got into some great arguments, but it was authentic personal interaction. No television. Of course, they didn't have computers back then or Gameboys, or all this kind of stuff. The interaction is critically important for development, for the kids' growing up, for their own self-acceptance, as well as for the development of intimacy within the development of the family.

It has been shown that adults who come from what used to be called broken homes, particularly men, find it almost impossible to get into a therapeutic relationship where they can be totally open. So you're going to come up with a Catch-22 situation where what you need to heal that is a therapeutic relationship, but you can't give yourself over to it.

+Jonah: Yes, in some cases the hurt is so deep there needs to be a therapeutic relationship with a trained therapist who knows how to skillfully and carefully reach into that pain and build a relationship with someone like that. One of the things that I really believe is important is to have trained professionals. A priest is a priest. Some people need a priest, and some need a psychologist. Some need a psychiatrist if they require medications. These are not bad things, they are all part of the healing community that can deal with certain aspects of our brokenness. There's this pietism in the Orthodox community in some places that says, "No, all you need is a priest, or some clairvoyant elder, and because of 'the grace of ordination' or whatever, they can take care of it." Well that's nonsense. Excuse me, but it's nonsense. If you have cancer, you don't go to an elder, you go to a doctor. And if he's good elder, he'll tell you to go to a doctor. We just finished reading in trapeza (the mealtime) the new biography of Elder Cleopa of Romania, this wonderful holy elder who reposed a couple of years ago. That's s a lot of the stuff that people would bring to him. Someone asked, "I'm sick, what should I do?" He said, "Go to a doctor!" The priest is there as a spiritual father, not a medical physician. So, it's important to have trained professions. For instance, I'm not a marriage counselor. I'm not a family counselor. I'm not a psychologist. I may think I am sometimes. I'm definitely an underpaid one, that's all I do sometimes. Sorry, it's true. But there are some things that are totally beyond my competence. If they need to handled by a professional who's trained in that area, that's what's necessary. It would be foolish and irresponsible of me to try to deal with something that is beyond my competence.

When you're dealing with something in which sacraments are involved, isn't a priest better than a psychologist?

+Jonah: Well, it depends on what you are talking about. If you want to get married you can go and have premarital counseling with a priest, if he is competent to do premarital counseling. But if you have major problems you may need a lot of work before you should get married. If this is the case, non-professional pre-marital counseling may not be adequate. The same thing applies within your marriage if there are problems. Yes, there are elements to take to your priest, like confession, but then you'll probably want somebody to facilitate communication between you and your wife, and help deal with whatever problems are there. If your priest is doing his job, he'll recommend a marriage and family counselor whom he trusts and whom he knows. He is not going to tell you, "Oh, you need to go see guru so and so." Ultimately, it is God who heals. Whether it's through a priest, whether it's through a psychologist, psychiatrist, whether it's through a brain surgeon, it doesn't matter. Whether it's through drugs, whether it's through therapy, whether it's through prayer. It is God who heals. God uses everything, and we need to take advantage of everything that He's given to us as a means of growth and healing. Now you don't want to go to a therapist who says you need to get rid of all that religion stuff. Or get divorced, and just "do what feels good"—that kind of thing. You want to go to someone who shares your same Christian values, who's going to tell you, well, maybe you need to learn to be patient and tough this out and deal with your own issues rather than simply blame your spouse because she makes you angry—the problem isn't your wife, the problem is your own issues and anger .

You talked about maybe looking for a Christian psychologist. Should you look for Christian medical doctors as well?

+Jonah: You need to look for a doctor who's most skilled for whatever malady you have. Quite frankly, if I have a brain tumor, I want the best brain surgeon there is, and not somebody who necessarily espouses one creed or another. Certain skill sets don't require adherence to a particular creed. But when you're dealing with something like psychology or psychiatry, you probably don't want somebody who's an atheist who thinks that faith is a delusion, damaging, or a psychological pathology, because they're dealing with your heart. And I think that's very important.

Can we open the discussion about parenting and what you were talking about, and what you should do with your children?

+Jonah: (Laughing) So, ask a monk about how to parent little children. Well, one thing that is very important is that guilt is not bad. There's unhealthy guilt, just like there's unhealthy shame, and there's very healthy shame that's very necessary. If you have a little kid who goes off and is in the habit of taking the silverware off the table and throwing it on the floor, well then you need to instruct the kid not to do that. They're going to feel guilty. And if they do it again, they're going to feel that guilt even without being punished. I personally don't have any problem with a gentle spanking in certain situations. Personally.

Some people say when there is a lack of punishment when the child is doing something wrong and he knows it, he thinks he's not loved because he's not punished.

+Jonah: Yes, even the Scriptures connect discipline with the love of parents and of God (Hebrews 12:5–11). On the other hand, there are very wrong kinds of punishment. It's very frustrating to have a bunch of young kids. It's very frustrating for example, for a woman alone with a bunch of young kids and the husband is off working 8–10 hours a day. There's no adult conversation, and no interaction, no support, and she becomes angry and it overflows on to the kids who are just being normal kids. So you've got to watch that. You've got to watch your reactions, lest they turn into punishment by rejection or abandonment. One of the most horrific and damaging things for a parent to say is, "I can't deal with you anymore, I'm going to go away. I don't want to be around you, I'm leaving." Think about what that does to a little kid, and how often we can be tempted to say something like that. I believe that produces scars that have to be repaired years later. One thing Kaufman talks about is, even when you've punished the child and the child is crying, still pick him up and hold him in your arms. Even when you're mad at him. Don't break the bridge, don't break the relationship. And even when you have to punish them, that doesn't mean that the relationship is broken. Some kids really need to get a swat once in awhile. Wake them up. Say, "NO, you can't do that." But that doesn't mean that once you swat them, you should emotionally abandon them.

This was my experience growing up. I was watched, adults watched me, and for the right reasons, I think. When it was obvious that I was transgressing, I was told, "OK, now you have to tell what you did, and how it was wrong." And if after two or three days I didn't bring forth some kind of repentance for it, they'd come in my room and we'd talk about that behavior. Then, my mom would actually say this, "I'm gonna whip you and this is gonna hurt me more than it's gonna hurt you," and there'd be tears in her face. Oftentimes she shed more tears than I did. Sometimes it would be, "I'm angry with you, so I can't punish you now. But when I'm done being angry, you're gonna be punished for it." Then the rule was that no one could leave the room until we hugged and kissed, after the punishment was administered. She'd sit there until I was ready to give her a hug and a kiss. That to me was just the best thing. I can recall a lot of spankings, but I can never recall being hit out of anger or anything that would resemble abuse.

I think it's really important to understand what abuse is. If you hit a child out of anger, then that's abuse. If you're out of control then that's abuse, and that's wrong. But corrective punishment, chastisement in total control, not to inflict pain, but to give a little physical reminder that that's wrong behavior and that behavior needs to change, that's a whole different thing. Sometimes you can talk to a little kid until you're blue in the face, and it isn't going to help. It's just not going to do much.

A person who is suffering from shame is the one who has a problem with initiating intimacy, but is the one who has to do it in order to start healing. What's some advice on how to initiate a healing relationship?

+Jonah: I think it's something that you can bring up in confession, if you have that kind of relationship with your father confessor, then begin there and develop that relationship. If you're married then talk about it with your spouse, talk about your fears, your needs. Or open up to a close friend. Somebody has to break the ice in beginning to create intimacy. Somebody has to open up first, and that's a big step. It can be a lot like jumping off into the deep end, especially if you're feeling very insecure and vulnerable and afraid to expose yourself. Even if someone else initiates the relationship, you still have to enter into it and take the risk of exposing yourself to being hurt again.

The reality is, the only way to start any kind of spiritual, emotional, or psychological healing is the hard way. There's no other way it's going to start or happen. It takes risk.

CHAPTER 8

Human Personhood and the Value of Suffering

"What is man that You are mindful of him, Or the son of man, that You take care of him? . . . Therefore, in all things He had to be made like His brethren . . . For in that He Himself has suffered, being tempted, He is able to aid those who are tempted" (Hebrews 2:6, 17–18).

Man is a great mystery. Human beings are crowned with glory and honor—created to be the very image of God. Every human being is an icon of God, a revelation of God, and filled with an infinite potential for growth in communion, for love.

The Scriptures tell us that God made man as the pinnacle of creation and put all things in subjection to him. This action, however, is seen as a process, not a point in time. It began with Adam, who named all creatures. It is still underway and will not be fulfilled until the Second Coming, when all things will be summed up in Christ and Christ gives over all things to the Father.

The Scriptures also tell us that man was created good by God. We bear the image of God as the defining element of our humanity. Part of that image is the potential to grow in likeness to God by our will and actions. Even though sin disrupts the fulfillment of that potential, we affirm that the potential is always there, that God's image is indelible. For this reason, the doctrine of "total depravity" of man is foreign to the understanding of the Orthodox Church.

Yet there is more to this story. Man's own being as the created image of God is not fulfilled until it is brought into union with the Uncreated Image of God, the Son. This is the essential process of creation itself: to move from potential to fulfillment. In Jesus, the created image and uncreated image of God come together, and in the Incarnation, through the human being, Mary, God becomes man. But yet, the process is still incomplete: Not only must Christ die and be resurrected, but the whole creation must be fulfilled in Him at the Second Coming. Until this time, the entire creation "groans and labors with birth pangs" (Romans 8:22).

For us, the process of union with Christ is the content of our salvation, which begins now and is only ultimately fulfilled when we are resurrected from the dead. But in this world, as we grow into the likeness of God by our cooperation with His will, by love, we actualize that potential here and now.

Made Perfect through Suffering

Jesus Christ is God become man. He is the revelation of the fulfillment of what it means to be a human being, both in His life by His words and deeds, and in His death by His Resurrection. He is the criterion of our knowledge of God, and of God's relationship to the world. Jesus did not simply come and teach about God. Rather, He revealed God by becoming a human being.

Jesus revealed God's love for us by His complete identification with us. He took on our full humanity, our complete nature. "He made Himself of no reputation, taking the form of a bondservant, and coming in the likeness of men." Then He "humbled Himself and became obedient to the point of death, even the death of the cross" (Philippians 2:7–8). By taking on not only our humanity, but our suffering and death, Jesus, who is the Incarnate Son and Word of God, shows God's love for man. To paraphrase the ancient Fathers, He became what we are that He might make us what He is.

St Paul says, "But we see Jesus, who was made a little lower than the angels, for the suffering of death crowned with glory and honor, that He, by the grace of God, might taste death for everyone. For it was fitting for Him, for whom are all things and by whom are all things, in bringing many sons to glory, to make the captain of their salvation perfect through suffering" (Hebrews 2:9–10).

How can it be that Jesus needed to be made perfect through suffering? It is because Jesus could not completely identify with us simply by assuming our human nature but not living our human life in the same flesh. He was not some kind of avatar (a deity temporarily taking on a human body), nor did He merely bear the resemblance of a man. Rather, He had to become completely what we are and share our life. He could not do that unless He shared also our suffering, and ultimately, our death.

What a marvel that God would humble Himself even to death, the most shameful death of the Cross! Jesus suffered and died as we suffer and die. But He overcame death and transformed it, so that we might no longer suffer from fear of death. He assumed our whole life and death, "that through death He might destroy him who had the power of death, that is, the devil, and release those who through fear of death were all their lifetime subject to bondage" (Hebrews 2:14–15).

Jesus not only revealed God's love for us by becoming man and teaching us about God. As the Incarnate Son, He has also become the human face of God who identifies with us in our suffering and temptations, having become like us in every respect including our pain and death. He revealed that God is not an abstract Being concealed in apophatic unapproachability, but is in reality a personal God who desires union with His creation which He loves.

Working Out Our Own Salvation

Christ has brought about salvation for us by identifying with us. We work out our salvation by identifying with Him. Our reception of His gift of Himself to us requires active participation on our part. Our salvation, our deification, is not something that happens passively in this world. There is no such thing as instant salvation, no "eternal security" once we have made some kind of an affirmation that we accept Christ's "atonement" for our sins.

Salvation is a process of continually identifying with Christ, a dynamic process that is mutual and reciprocal, it is "relationship." Jesus suffered that He might accompany us in our suffering. He was tempted that He might strengthen us when we are tempted. He overcame the fear of death that we might no longer be subject and in bondage to it. In this Jesus shows God's love and respect for us, for our freedom, for the integrity of our lives. He does not live our life for us, but rather has enabled us to live our life in Him, insofar as we will it.

Jesus did not come to eliminate suffering. Rather, He transformed it. Jesus was tempted, but He did not fall. He overcame the temptations that He might strengthen us to not succumb to temptation. He showed that suffering does not mean abandonment by God: Even on the Cross He remained faithful to God, and God remained faithful to Him, He was not left in the grave.

Jesus was faced with the temptation to reject His Cross. He chose rather to suffer, that His own suffering might work salvation for the whole world. Jesus transformed suffering into communion and overcame the power of temptation, so that we might have the strength to accept our own suffering as our cross and to overcome temptation.

Jesus came and suffered out of His love and compassion for us, so that we might learn to bear suffering as He bore it—as an act of compassion. This is what gives suffering meaning and value—it breaks the bonds of our selfishness and isolation from one another, so that we may truly love one another in compassion. We co-suffer with those who are suffering, that their suffering might not lead them into despair and death.

Suffering as an Act of Compassion

Suffering is inescapable in this fallen world. We suffer because of our own sins and those of others. We suffer because of death and grief, pain and separation, as victims and as perpetrators. We suffer as a result of our sinfulness, because of our selfishness and because we don't get our own way. This latter kind, suffering as a result of our own selfishness, is the first thing of which we need to be purified.

Temptation can be seen in terms of our willingness to suffer for the sake of the other, or to give in to our passions and selfishness and refuse to suffer with or for the other. Do we accept to suffer for the sake of helping someone, or do we let them be hurt? Do we accept to inconvenience ourselves, deny ourselves for the sake of the other? Will we accept to be reviled and persecuted, slandered and abused, and turn the other cheek? Or will we curse our abuser and give in to our anger, and thus fall into sin?

Will we accept the pain that sufferers inflict upon us in their frustration and distress, or will we cast them off to alleviate our own discomfort, or use drugs or alcohol to numb our conscience? Will we accept the burden of caring for the sufferers, or will we cast off the cross of love and compassion for the sake of an easy solution: Drug them up, send them to a nursing home (and let someone else worry about them), or simply kill them ("euthanasia"). Will we accept the suffering of the shame of being an unwed mother, as did the Virgin Mary, or simply abort the life of the infant before the pregnancy shows?

Temptation, on the deeper levels, is not about gratification of our passions. It is the temptation to cast off the cross, to refuse to suffer for the sake of the other, and to refuse the responsibility that love of neighbor demands.

Jesus Himself was tempted in the desert by the devil (Luke 4). He accepted to suffer hunger rather than turn stones to bread. He was tempted to settle for earthly glory and a temporal kingdom. Finally, the devil tempted Him simply to show His power as Messiah, cast Himself from the pinnacle of the temple, and be instantly declared king, thus refusing the way of the Cross to the eternal Kingdom.

In the garden, Jesus was tempted again. He asked if the cup of suffering could pass Him by, but ultimately He surrendered Himself to the will of God. Jesus helps us in our temptations by showing us that, when we accept to suffer for the sake of doing the will of God, when we accept our cross, our suffering is unto salvation. He stands by us and empowers us, energizes us by grace, to bear whatever cross we have been given. Suffering voluntarily by refusing to give in to temptation becomes an act of communion, and thus we become like Him.

Our secular materialist and hedonistic culture lives in denial of suffering. It sees it as essentially meaningless, as something to be alleviated as quickly and thoroughly as possible, and at all costs. Thus our medical establishment has not only found cures for innumerable diseases and maladies, but has developed medications to anesthetize all kinds of psychic pain as well. There is not necessarily anything wrong with this in all cases. But—and this is very important—this has led to an inability to cope with any kind of pain and suffering. We look for a quick solution in a pill or bottle, and alleviate the symptoms while leaving the underlying causes intact. Hence the rampant substance abuse in our culture; hence the nursing homes and endless retirement facilities to which we banish our elders; hence abortion and euthanasia.

This inability to bear suffering only leads to greater suffering in the long run. We look for political solutions to social ills and injustices, and fail to exercise any kind of personal compassion. We would rather send a check. We justify our selfishness by claiming that our elders would be better cared for "by professionals." We refuse to deal with the sufferings—age, disease, disability—of even our closest family members by institutionalizing them and forgetting their existence, while ignoring the fact that the most important thing they need is our love. Even death itself is vainly hidden and its reality denied in a grotesque masquerade by the commercial funeral industry.

Co-Sufferers with Christ

The calling of Christians is to learn authentic love and compassion, literally "co-suffering." We must learn how to bear suffering so that we can identify ourselves with those who are suffering, accompany them and raise them up. "Greater love has no man than this, that a man lay down his life for his friends" (Jn. 15:13). By learning to co-suffer, to have compassion, to truly lay down our life for the other, we identify ourselves with Christ and actualize the likeness to God that is the very fulfillment of our personhood. In other words, we learn to love unselfishly and unconditionally, as He does.

St Paul says, "Suffering produces endurance, and endurance produces character, and character produces hope, and hope does not disappoint us, because God's love has been poured into our hearts through the Holy Spirit which has been given to us" (Romans 5:3–5, RSV).

Suffering has meaning. It is the means by which we grow, by which we become authentically ourselves through attaining likeness to Christ, who suffered and died for us. By enduring suffering ourselves, we attain to perseverance and character. We begin to understand our sins and temptations. We learn to take responsibility for our lives and our sins, blaming neither God nor our neighbor. We purify ourselves by refusing to give in to temptation, and strengthen our will so that we remain in communion with God. Suffering purifies us, if we let it, because it reveals our selfishness to us so that we can repent.

The Way of the Cross

We can either accept to suffer in compassion and bear our cross, or give in to our own selfishness. To suffer for the sake of compassion lets the energy of God's grace and love be poured into our heart so that we enter into synergy with that grace through our actions. This kind of compassion is not simply human, but it is divine as well. This is the very process of deification. We are thus given the strength to raise up those who are suffering, because by our perseverance in co-suffering, we attain to hope.

When we allow our suffering to lead us into despair and desolation, we become so turned in on ourselves that we reject God and the compassion of others. The Fathers of the Church see this as a kind of foretaste of hell. We torment ourselves by our rejection of our true self, which can only be fulfilled by communion in love with God and the other. God's love is not diminished, but we vainly refuse to accept it by refusing to forgive ourselves and others.

Thus, the fire of the love of God burns us. Our self-torment feels like punishment, the wrath of God. But it is not God's punishment, as we often think. Rather, it is the fruit of our own self-obsession, self-hatred and our self-rejection. This kind of suffering is meaningless, leading nowhere. It is the essence of nihilism, of suicide.

Suffering takes on meaning when we accept to endure it and allow ourselves to be transformed by it. This seems an enormous task, especially for one in the grips of pain and depression. But the only way through it is to come out of ourselves and accept the compassion of others, who strengthen us by their co-suffering in love. First and foremost is the remembrance of Christ's own co-suffering with us by enduring the Cross for us. He endured His Cross so that we can endure ours. By the power of His Cross, we have hope—hope that our suffering will lead us to and be fulfilled in our salvation.

PART II

One Holy, Catholic and Apostolic Church

CHAPTER 9

The Orthodox
Church in America

VISION, VOCATION,
MISSION, IDENTITY

(Divine Ascent No. 11, Lent 2008)

The Holy Spirit gives the Church her vision, which comes from our identity in Christ as His Body. This vision is identical with the vision of all those who have gone before us precisely because it is the same Body, with the same vocation, mission, and identity: to be the Body of Christ: the One, Holy, Catholic, and Apostolic Church. Whenever we add elements to that vision, we distort it, no matter how noble our qualifications and agendas may be. Whenever we subtract from or diminish it, we do likewise. If we change the vision in any way, we exclude ourselves from it and from the Body which it constitutes.

Taking Responsibility and Repenting

There is a lot of interest in the sad scandals that are plaguing the Orthodox Church in America, in the East and in the North. Dire warnings of doom, betrayals, and speculations of perverse motives are all over the internet and discussed widely. In particular, much is being said and written to the effect that the OCA lacks vision and that this, in turn, is due to a lack of good leadership.

Such talk points to a truth: It is certainly the task of our ecclesiastical leaders constantly to announce and renew the Church's vision. But how, exactly, is this to happen? Is there a specifically churchly way to go about this task? For we are not a corporation or secular organization, and in this instance we cannot have recourse to secular models. Our identity, vocation, and mission—both as individual members of the Church and together as the one Body of the Church—derive from the Church's vision. Her vision is not that of any particular leader but is shared by the whole Body of the faithful.

Our task is to turn away from our own petty individual worlds, causes, and dreams—the delusions of our own reasonings. And our leaders' task is constantly to call us back to this repentance. This they must do so that we can share the vision given by the grace of the Holy Spirit and accept our calling from Christ to be the Church, His Body, which constitutes the very core of our personal and corporate identity.

But when this leadership fails to occur—when our leaders do not call us to repentance by word and example, but instead cause scandal, sorrow, and pain—what then? For undoubtedly there has been egregious wrongdoing, and these matters are serious and profoundly affect the lives of many. Thus there is a tremendous need for healing and for restoration of confidence.

When one is suffering, all suffer together. When one member is honored, all rejoice (cf. 1 Corinthians 12:26). This is the basic principle of our communion in Christ. The bishops have a particular kind of responsibility, but they are not the Church by themselves; nor are the clergy, nor the rest of the laity. How do we support our bishops so that they can bear their portion of responsibility for the life of the whole Body? Christ is calling us to take the responsibility for the Church that is already ours by virtue of our baptism and chrismation. It's not about how "they" deal with it. It's about us. It's our life, our union in Christ with one another.

If there is a lack of accountability and transparency in the hierarchy, is it not our responsibility to correct it? How would it have arisen, had we not abrogated our responsibility to demand integrity from the very leaders we put into office? If we judge those in positions of authority who have fallen, we only accuse and judge ourselves. It is easier to blame hypocritically than simply to accept the responsibility of cleaning up the mess. We should grieve over our brothers' sins, not judge them. And in so doing, we come together in compassion. This strengthens our unity and welds us together in a common task: to take responsibility for the life of our Church.

Authority is responsibility. When authority degenerates into power, egoism, and position, it destroys the image of Christ which those positions of responsibility are meant to depict. "Whoever would be first among you must be slave of all" (Mark 10:44). The chief pastors of the Church are called to be that image of Christ, as are all of us the faithful. They fall short; we fall short. But we must constantly return in repentance, and encourage our fathers and brethren in that same repentance, supporting those who bear the responsibility for our souls. It is a heavy burden. But if we all bear it together, in a synergy of love and communion, it becomes the easy yoke and light burden of Christ, in Christ, by Christ. When we try to bear it by ourselves in isolation, we will inevitably fall, because it becomes something outside of Christ, about our own ego.

Thus, we must not become despondent or fearful. Instead, we must repent as a body. We must turn towards God and away from the abstractions of petty personal agendas, which can include a vindictive and worldly desire for the punishment of those who have offended us. We must not be blind to our own sin and corruption. "Let him who is without sin cast the first stone" (John 8:7). We must open our minds and hearts to Jesus Christ and to one another. Then we will see with great clarity the vision of the Church of Christ, and this will show us how to set our house in order, cleaning up the mess that we as a body have allowed.

The Vision of the Kingdom

So, what is the vision of the Orthodox Church in America, and thus her identity, vocation, and mission? It is nothing other than Jesus Christ and His Kingdom. This vision is revealed to us when we celebrate the Eucharist, and the Eucharist, in turn, sends us on our mission: to bring Christ's Gospel to America in all its Orthodox integrity. We do not need the ways of the corporate world (vision and mission brainstorming, etc.) to determine this. Rather, we need prayer and discernment—together as the body of the Church, and in particular on the part of our Holy Synod of archbishops and bishops—in order to renew the vision of the Kingdom and to preach and proclaim the unity that exists in Christ by the Holy Spirit and constitutes us as the Church.

This vision is not about programs, institutions, administrations, budgets, or bureaucrats. Even less is it about the personal ambitions, agendas, or self-aggrandizements of bishops, clergy, lay leaders, or anyone else. It is only about Jesus Christ and His Kingdom. All the concrete projects we undertake, all the offices and positions of authority and responsibility, flow from this source. "Seek first the Kingdom of God and His righteousness and all these things shall be yours as well" (Matthew 6:33).

If as an organization we had lost our vision, then we would have ceased to be the Church. But this is not the case here. That vision, and the grace to actualize and incarnate it, is bestowed at every Eucharist.

The blessed and ever-memorable Father Alexander Schmemann clearly saw and clearly articulated the Kingdom of God, imparted in the Eucharist, as the focal point of the Church's life. It was this clarity of vision which gave such great strength to his leadership. We need to get back in touch with that vision. We must return to our first love. It is the Liturgy that gives us our identity and sends us on our mission, renewing our vocation to be the Body of Christ—the One, Holy, Catholic, and Apostolic Church in the world.

The Marks of the Church

The Church's four characteristic "marks"—unity, holiness, catholicity, and apostolicity—are at once the Church's content and identity, constituting both her vocation and mission. They are our goal; it is our challenge to actualize them in our lives, both personally and corporately, in order for us to be the Church.

Before anything else, these characteristics are marks of Christ Himself. Jesus Christ is one with the Father and the Holy Spirit; He is the focal point of our unity, and the very context of our relationship with God and one another as His Body. Jesus is the ultimate criterion of holiness: the man transparent to God, revealing God, incarnating God, and imparting that holiness which is participation in God's very life, which lifts us up from the world of sin and corruption. Christ is the essence of catholicity or wholeness, in that "all things were created through Him and for Him . . . and in Him all things hold together" (Colossians 1:16–17). He is also the source of universality because He embraces all things and permeates all things, and all things exist in Him. And He is the foundation of apostleship, the apostle and high priest from God (Hebrews 3:1), whose obedience reveals Him as transparent to God, speaking only the words of Him who sent Him (John 3:34), and doing whatever He sees the Father do (John 5:19), transforming and redeeming the world.

Our vision as Orthodox Christians is always first and foremost Jesus Christ. His message is our message: the coming of the Kingdom. His life is our life. His mission is our mission: the salvation of all mankind and its union with the Father in Christ by the Holy Spirit. Our task in the midst of this is constantly to repent, to have this vision renewed in us, and to purge our lives of everything contrary to the vision and incarnation of Christ in our lives. These are the marks of Christ; and if we share His life, we also share these marks.

The Role of Autocephaly

The unity, sanctity, catholicity, and apostolicity of the Orthodox Church cannot be the exclusive possession of Middle-Eastern, Mediterranean and Slavic countries and peoples. The Orthodox Church in America has the vocation to manifest all the fullness of Christ's Church here in America. Her autocephaly was sought and granted in 1970 precisely to facilitate this. Many today look on that event as a grave mistake, the sad fruits of which we are now forced to reap. But if we make the effort to build up and not to tear down (1

Corinthians 3:10), a more constructive approach to our autocephaly becomes apparent.

For, in fact, the greatest strength of the Orthodox Church in America is that in her we have taken full responsibility for the life and integrity of our Church and do not rely on anyone anywhere else. Of course, we preserve sisterly relations and Eucharistic communion with the other Orthodox Churches. But we elect our own bishops, we oversee our own finances, and we support our own ministries. None of the other Orthodox communities in America can say that. Thus we are responsible for our own mistakes, as well as our own victories. And when we are faced with a problem, we are responsible, as a single Body in Christ, to deal with it in a Christ-like manner. Yes, we sin; and the sins of one, ultimately, belong to all of us—the healing and reconciliation of those who have been hurt by sin are the responsibility of us all.

Therefore, our problems will not be solved by someone from the outside. No one overseas can come to the rescue. No one will impose one more set of foreign ecclesiastical bureaucrats answerable only to a distant despot somewhere in the Old World. Thank God. This is the beauty and the responsibility of autocephaly. It is our great strength. We simply need to put aside the distractions of our passions and accept this responsibility given by God: to be the Orthodox Church in this country; to reveal the presence of Jesus Christ here in America to souls perishing in darkness, ignorance, and despair; to give them hope; and to lead them to repentance in the knowledge and love of God.

CHAPTER 10

Where Do We Go from Here?

(*Divine Ascent* No. 10, Summer 2005)

Father Alexander Schmemann: In Memoriam

Over twenty years have passed since the repose of Father Alexander Schmemann. Father Alexander's vision shaped the structure and life of the Orthodox Church in America as well as St Vladimir's Seminary. His works informed and infuriated, transformed and influenced the life of the whole Orthodox community in America and beyond.

Reading his works now, I am impressed not only by his vision, but by how far the Church has come over the past fifty years since Father Alexander came to the United States from France. No longer is lay non-participation in the Eucharist the norm, a huge transformation. No longer is it questioned that the liturgical texts are a primary access to the Mind of the Church. The liturgy in the OCA is universally served in English, or the language of the local community where necessary. No longer is the OCA a Slavic ghetto of ex-Uniates; it has become a truly catholic community based on faith rather than ethnic and family tradition. No longer is it canonically isolated; it is fully in communion with all the other Orthodox Churches. Great numbers of the clergy, many of whom are converts to Orthodoxy, are well educated with master's degrees in divinity or theology. These were some of the main issues with which Father Alexander dealt.

There are still more issues, however, which remain unresolved. The question of the so-called "diaspora" and the role of the Ecumenical Patriarchate is a key issue, which not only Father Alexander but many others courageously addressed. The OCA's autocephaly remains unaccepted by Constantinople, though its canonicity is unquestioned. Most of all, his vision of a united American Orthodox Church, embracing all Orthodox Christians under a single hierarchy, fully autocephalous and engaged with the contemporary social and cultural milieu, remains unfulfilled.

Father Alexander delineated some of the key challenges that the Orthodox Church must face in its mission in this culture. One such challenge is secularization: the reduction of Orthodoxy to a compartmentalized religious form fulfilling people's "religious needs," while their overall worldview remains defined by "the world." Father Alexander wrote against this sellout to secularization, and it is one of the greatest impacts on how we do mission in our culture.

Another central issue is the relationship of monasticism to the mission of the Orthodox Church in this culture. At the time of Father Alexander's death, monasticism was very minimal in North America. The larger men's monasteries were primarily outside the canonical churches, and some were riddled with scandal. Others preserved external forms, but they sorely lacked elders with profound spiritual maturity. Still others were barely nascent, or even experimental in their forms and expression. Monasticism was entirely marginal to the life of the Orthodox community in America (except perhaps in the Russian Church Abroad). Elder Ephraim's communities were not even planned. Father Alexander took a rather dim view of monasticism, undoubtedly because of its spiritual shallowness and external religiosity, as well as his knowledge of the corruption just under the surface of so many communities. He rejected the pharisaical externalism that is such an easy temptation for monasticism, the anti-intellectualism and arrogant elitism, all of which were part of the corruption of monasticism in Romanov Russia. Some say that his attitude was a carry-over from the rivalry between white and black clergy imbedded in the Russian ecclesiastical community. My opinion is that he would have agreed entirely with St Ignatiy Brianchaninov, that where monasticism is in line with the Gospel it is healthy and constructive. Where it is formal and external, it is useless.

Since Father Alexander's death, the Orthodox Church in America has suffered a crisis in vision. Father Alexander had provided that vision and direction, but no successors have arisen to his role of leadership. We have to ask the question, "Where do we go from here?" There is consensus that there is a crisis in vision and leadership. Given the foundation of Father Alexander's work, what will bring us back to a unified vision and direction as we strive to do the work of mission as the Orthodox Church in America? We must first examine the past few years, and evaluate the context we have to address, before trying to answer this question.

Where Do We Go from Here?

The mission of the Orthodox Church in North America has come a long way over the past forty years, with the formation of SCOBA, the autocephaly of the OCA, the influx of converts and translation of the services, the reconciliation of the Ukrainian Churches in North America with the Ecumenical Patriarchate, the relative autonomy of the Antiochian Archdiocese, and soon, the healing of the schism between ROCOR and the Russian Mother Church. The face of the Orthodox Church has changed dramatically, with the publication of literature, the education of clergy to better minister to the people, and the establishment of monasticism on a broad scale. But the question, and the point of judgment and hence the crisis, is, Where do we go from here?

We cannot make light of any of the remarkable developments of the past years. But we are faced with an ever changing social and political situation which is leaving our churches in a rather strange predicament. The old established social institutions—the Protestant churches which were the ethnic churches of American culture—are changing so rapidly that they have lost their Christian vision and validate all sorts of immorality. They have lost their status as defining elements in American culture and morality, and have are fast becoming post-Christian, dying on the vine. The new Evangelical and Pentecostal churches are attracting large crowds, but there is little staying power. People usually remain members for no more than three years. These churches have a lot of excitement and entertainment, but the experience is often very shallow and unsatisfying. They emphasize the Bible, but preach an oversimplified and distorted Calvinism or some other strange idea, and are blown about by every wind of doctrine. Fundamentalism means either dispensationalism, Calvinism or whatever the preacher has been reading that week. The Roman Catholic Church is being battered by these same social currents, and hangs onto its orthodoxy by the strength of the papacy alone, whose authority is steadily declining in the American scene. There is theological, liturgical, and spiritual chaos. And on top of that is the ever growing New Age conglomeration of syncretisms. Then, you have us.

To paraphrase Father Thomas Hopko, from the inside, the Orthodox Church seems absolutely crazy. Until you look at the churches outside. Then we seem to be the paragon of stability. Orthodoxy in America has been shielded by its ethnicism and inherent conservatism from some of these social trends. It was even the most rapidly growing denomination in the country for a while. But, as the Church becomes indigenous in this country, it is encountering and has to deal with the culture at large. It can no longer hide under the dark veils of mystical antiquity and languages incomprehensible even to the faithful. Babushka watches Pat Robertson and Mother Angelica. Yaya watches Benny Hinn. Our people are now well educated and sophisticated businessmen, no longer non-English speaking immigrants. And thousands of converts have flooded the churches across the jurisdictional spectrum, each with his own baggage.

On one hand, the liturgy remains the same—though substantially in English—and there is no interest in changing it or the theology behind it. Church life remains the same, with festivals, bible studies, and dance and choral groups. Things are comfortable. But if we are going to go beyond where we are now, we are going to have to change. Not the liturgy or other services: They are a given. No one is interested in a reformation or Vatican II for Orthodoxy. Not even the day to day life of the parish or diocese will change. What must change is our fundamental attitude about who we are and what we are doing, and how we go about doing it. It is a question of vision and of mission.

For too long, we have been concerned about simply maintaining "our" church, serving "our" people, focusing on the services and on social events. But we have sorely neglected the core of the Gospel: to bring the good news to the poor, to heal the brokenhearted, to give sight to the blind and to raise the fallen. We have served mostly ourselves, and anyone who wants to join us—but not "Them." This is not what our Lord Jesus Christ has given us to do. He has commissioned us to "Go into all the world, preach the Gospel to every nation, baptizing them . . . teaching them to observe all I have commanded" (Matt 28:19–20). Our vision has been constricted, and our mission has been curtailed into something self-serving. We are so concerned about our own visions and missions, consisting of the petty little agendas of our organizations, that we ignore the underlying mission of the Gospel. It is no wonder that there are multiple parallel jurisdictions. We have lost sight of the thing that really unifies us: the vision and mission of the Gospel.

So what is the Gospel? What is the Good News that we have for people? We have lots of news for people, and lots of invitations, but they are not necessarily very good.

The Gospel is not that Orthodoxy is the True Religion and all the rest are false. The Gospel is not that they can become born-again Russians, Ukrainians, Greeks, Syrians, Serbs or what have you. It is not that they can come help us pay the mortgage. It is not that they can support our position against the Others—like the OCA vs. the Ecumenical Patriarchate, or Antioch vs. Jerusalem, or God only knows what. It is not that they can come join some enclave of a foreign culture and even be (more or less) accepted.

The Only Agenda: The Gospel

If we are really Orthodox, we should be able to preach the Gospel better than anyone else, because we have it in an undistorted form. So what is it?

First and foremost that Jesus Christ is risen from the dead, trampling death by death and giving life to those in the tombs. It is the message of the Resurrection, the victory of Jesus Christ over death and hell. It is the Good News that the Kingdom of God is present, here and now, by the grace of the Holy Spirit, and you can be baptized into it, commune of its grace, and be filled with new life. It is this that we constantly celebrate in church, in the services, in the cycles of feasts and fasts. And what does it do for us? It heals our souls, and raises us up from despair, and enables us to deal with any obstacle that comes in our way.

The good news of the "Orthodox" Gospel is that we are free from the destructive perversions of the Gospel which pervade the religious presuppositions of our post-Christian ex-Protestant culture. We don't preach that God is a harsh judge waiting to damn us to hell for the least transgression. How often do we say in the Liturgy, "For You are a good God and the lover of mankind," or "You are a God of mercy and compassion and love for mankind." This is Good News. We don't preach that we are inescapably predestined to be saved or damned, and there is not a thing we can do about it, either way. And we don't preach that being a Christian is about going to heaven when we die. What do we say? As St John Chrysostom said, "For You have brought us up to heaven and endowed us with your kingdom which is to come." Here and now, not just when we're dead. And we don't need to forget those who have gone before us, but we have continual remembrance of them, because in Christ they are alive with the same life with which we also live.

We celebrate the Sunday of Orthodoxy, but it needs to be a real celebration of the integrity of the Gospel message. The triumph over iconoclasm has an essential point of faith: by His Incarnation, Jesus Christ sanctified matter. We can paint a picture of God Incarnate, and experience His Presence in and through venerating the icon. We can partake of His life by eating the bread and wine of His Body and Blood; we are immersed into His life in Baptism, anointed with the Holy Spirit in Chrismation, and made part of His Body. The world itself, matter, is sanctified by Christ's Coming, and becomes a means of communion with God. And we ourselves, in this body, in this life, here and now, are sanctified and made holy, partakers of the life of God. Salvation is about life here and now, not "fire insurance" for after death! In Christ, all things are made new. "For He has brought us up to heaven, and endowed us with His Kingdom which is to come." This is Good News!

A Call to Repentance

So what do we need to do? We need to focus on this life-giving message of the Gospel, which is what the Church, its life and services, are about anyway. We need to surrender to Christ, and put aside our self-serving agendas. Only then can we come together to do the work of Christ: to draw all people to Him. We need to learn the Scripture, so that we can live it. We need to serve the poor and those in need without regard to who they are or whether they are "ours." In short, we need to love our neighbor as our self. In other words, it is time that we accepted the responsibility to incarnate the message of Christ at all costs. It is time we grew up.

Orthodoxy in North America has come a long way. Our forefathers in the Faith have laid a foundation for us to build upon. It is here that we can be encouraged and informed by the vision of Father Alexander Schmemann, and others. We have a lot of work to do and we have a long way to go. We must repent of the sins and attitudes which have distorted the life of our Church here, and then tear down the obstacles we have erected to fulfilling the mission of the Gospel.

We have to repent of ethnic phyletism. This includes convertism as well. I do not mean that our communities will not have their own traditional flavors—in more ways than one! We have to rejoice in our diversity; but not at the expense of our unity and cooperation. We can't let any human barriers get in the way of the Gospel: language, culture, social or economic status, race, or anything else. When we let any human category exclude others from the Church, we sell out Christ, as the Jews did who refused to let Gentiles enter the Church.

We have to repent of the exclusiveness that leads us into sectarianism and self-enclosure in our own little self-satisfied groups. This attitude is alien to the Catholic mind, which presupposes a holistic vision of the faith and community of the Church. This means authentic encounter with non-Orthodox Christians in a spirit of humility and openness, not insecurity and arrogance. Exclusivist sectarianism is not the vision of the Catholic Church of the Roman Empire that embraced hundreds of cultures and united them in Christ. It doesn't matter what the rituals look like if we do not have a Catholic vision. If we are not Catholic, we are not Orthodox.

We have to assert that we are not in diaspora. We have been here for many generations, and our churches are consecrated to last until the Second Coming. We are Americans and Canadians, with heritages to be proud of. We rejoice in our communion with the Churches of the Old World, but we are Orthodox Christians here and now, and we need to govern our own affairs and elect our own bishops and primate. The Fathers have taught us that as Christians we can have no abiding earthly country. We are citizens of the Kingdom of Heaven.

Orthodox churches can only be organized canonically on the basis of local territorial boundaries. We have to end the parallel jurisdictions, which fundamentally distort the life and mission of the Church. The most important canonical objection the Orthodox have against the Papacy is its assertion of universal jurisdiction, without territorial boundaries. Yet we have fallen into the same heresy, as virtually every national Orthodox church has jurisdiction outside its territorial borders, as in America. Just look at a phone book. We have to remind our hierarchs that there is no such thing as "universal jurisdiction" in the Orthodox Church, so if we are to continue to consider ourselves within the Apostolic Tradition, things must change.

Repentance entails not only recognizing and admitting the sin. It is not fulfilled until the sin is overcome, not to be repeated. This means that we have to reorganize the life of the Church in North America, with one synod of all the Orthodox bishops, under one primate elected by them. This is the only way to bring an end to the confusion and competition between the jurisdictions, all of whom are doing the same thing, but are captive to foreign nationalistic agendas. The mission of the Church in America must not be held hostage to the agendas of patriarchs and synods thousands of miles away in different cultures and nations. If they could be convinced to relinquish their tight hold on their American cash cows, they might find our financial support of them to increase.

Still more important, however, is the critical need to repent of our self-serving agendas, which reinforce parochial and jurisdictional isolation and competition. If we could focus on the needs of the local community around us, and not just on ourselves and our institutions, every financial need and every personnel shortage would resolve itself. We must simply open our doors and hearts to those in need: those held by the poverty of loneliness and isolation, as well as financial need; those suffering from addictions and abuse; the thousands of children needing a safe place to go after school; the women—the widows of our age, from loss or divorce—left abandoned and in poverty barely able to survive. To minister to them is to preach the Gospel in words far stronger than any rhetoric. To receive them in love incarnates the Gospel, and fulfills the church as the Body of Christ—for "they will know you are my disciples by how you love one another" (cf. John 13: 35).

On a more subtle level there is another temptation which demands our repentance. Too often we reduce the life of the Church to the services, to the cult, to religion. Those of us who are priests and concerned with the integrity and beauty of the services are especially prone to this. The Church is not the services. The Church is not the Eucharist. The Eucharist constitutes and fulfills the Church, but it is there to constitute and fulfill the entire life of the whole community, its good works of charity and self-denial, the self-offering of the faithful to those in need. But if these things are forgotten, what does the Eucharist consecrate and fulfill? It simply becomes a ritual act to fulfill the "religious needs" of the people.

Father Alexander Schmemann drew a sharp distinction between religion and faith. How easy it is to be religious—to focus on the external dimensions of the life of the church, its services, rules, disciplines, aesthetics, structure. But if these become ends in themselves, rather than expressions and supports to a life of faith manifest in works of charity, then our trust in these things is in vain and we are hypocrites, "having the form of religion but denying its power" (cf. 2 Tim 3:5). As one abbot recently said, "It's hard not to be a Pharisee when you look like one!" It is not the forms that are the problem, but rather, our attitude towards them and the focus of our life as a Christian community. We are called to "do the one without neglecting the other."

The reduction of faith to observance of religious forms is a foundational element of secularization. The forms divorced from their content become meaningless, or at best nostalgic reminders of bygone days. They can thus be compartmentalized or discarded, having no real impact on how we live our lives. The only way to fight secularization is to emphasize that faith is about how we live our life: not only the remembrance of God, but how we treat other people, for how we treat our neighbor is the criterion of how we love God. In this way, our faith is not relegated to an hour or so on Sunday morning. Rather, it impacts every encounter with another person, and every relationship we have.

Our communion with our neighbor is the criterion of our faith. The agendas of power and money, organizations and institutions, by which we isolate ourselves from our neighbors, are ultimately distractions from our real vocation as the Church. Our real calling is the mission given us by Christ, the work of Christ himself: "To preach the good news to the poor, to heal the broken hearted, to preach deliverance to captives and the recovery of sight to the blind, to set at liberty those who are oppressed, to proclaim the acceptable year of the Lord" (Luke 4:18). Then our religion will be true and authentic: "Pure and undefiled religion before God and the Father is this: to visit orphans and widows in their trouble, and to keep oneself unspotted from the world" (James 1:27).

Eucharistic Life: Thanksgiving with Joy

As Father Alexander would remind us, the most essential elements of the Christian life are joy and thanksgiving. When we live a life of faith, overcoming our selfishness by self-denial, doing the works of charity for which we have been recreated in Christ, we can have no other attitude but joy, and we offer all things to God in a sacrifice of thanksgiving. We sin and fall short—but repenting, we find joy. We have to bear our cross, whatever it may be; but "behold, through the cross, joy has come into all the world!" We have great and diverse elements within our communities; but we can rejoice in the unity of the Spirit, as one Body.

What is our vocation as the Church but to be witnesses to the world of Christ's resurrection, to heal by our love, and to raise the whole world as an offering of thanksgiving to God? Then all our life, as persons and as community, is transformed into a Eucharistic celebration of joy, an anticipation of the Presence of Christ in His Kingdom.

CHAPTER 11

Creativity and Tradition

(*Divine Ascent* No. 7, Presentation of the Theotokos 2001)

"In what is necessary, unity; in what is dubious, diversity; in all things, charity." —St Augustine of Hippo

Creativity is inherent within the Tradition, as synergy vivified by the energy of the Holy Spirit. It is the power that fuels the continual growth of the life of the Church, and its adaptation to each new cultural environment. This is active within individual members of the Church, as each one personally embraces the new life communicated by grace. This divine creativity is active within communities and churches, as each particular congregation incarnates the universal Church. The saint, one who has attained "a measure of the stature of the fullness of Christ" (Ephesians 4:13), is one who has been transformed in synergy with divine grace. A church is fulfilled by its liturgical synergy, each with the others in Christ by the Holy Spirit, in communion. Both are the transformation of life—human life, the life of the creation, the life of the community—into the mystery of the presence of the Kingdom of God on earth. The inner dimension of this is the personal ascent into communion with God by purification and illumination, individually and corporately. The external dimension and expression of this movement draws all men into that same mystery of communion. This double action of the Spirit, inwards and outwards, is the core of the living Tradition, as we are drawn by God into this cosmic and Divine Liturgy.

The personal and corporate dimensions of our life in the Spirit, and the inward and outward directions of that movement, are a profoundly creative process. On the personal level, creativity is needed to adapt one's life to the forms and traditions of the Church. But on a far deeper level, creativity rooted in synergy with grace, the process of purification, illumination and deification, motivates us as we confront our lives in the light of the living Presence of Christ.

On the corporate level, those forms which developed as means of conveying the experience of faith in Christ, both liturgical and institutional, evolved in particular cultures and times. While some forms remain stable, such as the canon of Scripture or the text of the Liturgy, the ways they are expressed and interpreted—ritual forms, institutional forms—evolve and develop as people strive in communion with Christ and one another to communicate the Gospel creatively. Without this, the forms and traditions are empty, and are simply hypocrisy with no saving value. Yet to the degree that we are involved in the great process of creative spiritual transformation, both personally and corporately, the forms and traditions are fulfilled as guides to that new life. It is the spirit of the law, not the letter that counts; yet we must fulfill the one without neglecting the other.

The personal and the corporate dimensions are in no way separate, though they are distinct. Each person must undergo the process of spiritual transformation individually through repentance and conversion. Yet, the context for this, the only context, is the community of the Church, and its liturgy of life, its procession into the Kingdom. The more thorough and intense the process is for each member, the deeper and richer the life of the whole community will be. Much has been written on the personal process of transformation in Christ. Here, we need to explore the corporate dimension of that creative process, and its implications for the institutional forms of the Church in our own cultural context.

The Liturgy is the locus where the particular community is fulfilled as Church by itself becoming the Body of Christ. The many are united in one by the Holy Spirit, in the great movement of love and self-offering to the Father of the one Christ, head and body. The Liturgy is the focal point of the revelation of the Church as the Kingdom of God, just as communion is the focal point for each of the faithful for their personal transcendence of themselves, and their realization of their true identity as members of the Body of Christ. At this instant the personal ascetic striving and the corporate ascent coincide, intersect, and are fulfilled. It is not the case, however, that the mystery of the Church is only manifested in the eucharistic Liturgy. The sanctification of the life of the community itself, daily life, is also a fundamental element of the Church as the revelation of the Kingdom of God on earth.

The life of each community of the Church is built around the mutual support of the members for one another in their common spiritual process of transformation. This, of course, is most obvious in a monastic community. But it must also be the content of all communities of the Church. This process requires tremendous creativity: learning to deal with one another, each with a different level of spiritual, emotional, and personal maturity and experience, not to mention different characters, bearing one another's burdens, and sharing a common vision and goal. Each aspect of this has a transcendent, as well as personal, dimension. Every interaction, no matter how mundane, has an impact on the life of the community as a body, manifesting either mutual love in Christ, or the selfishness of the world. If the members are fighting among themselves, what kind of Liturgy are they going to celebrate?

The communities of the Church are made up of people from a particular place and time, with a particular culture. It is pure pretense—delusion—for them to try to be anything else. The task of the Church is to sanctify that particular culture, and those particular people, making their community transparent to the Kingdom of God, and to reveal the reality of God's transforming Presence to the other people in that particular place and time and culture. A Christian community reveals the mystery of the Kingdom of God in the midst of the world, transfiguring and deifying the particular persons by grace, baptizing the particular culture, language, and forms as means of communicating that grace and the Gospel of the Kingdom. "In the church I would rather speak five words with my understanding, that I may teach others also, than ten thousand words in a tongue" (1 Corinthians 14:19).

To bring this down to concrete terms, we must ask ourselves what our institutions, our parish communities and organizations, our liturgy and our lives, communicate to the people around us. Are we communicating the Gospel and salvation, or simply the external forms of "religion"? Are our institutions, activities, and organizations effective in communicating to us and supporting us in our common process of repentance and conversion, purification and illumination? Do we authentically love one another—the only mark of the disciples of the Lord Jesus? Are our communities icons of the Kingdom of God, communicating life in Christ? And further, how can we creatively engage the Tradition and our own culture, in view of our personal and corporate spiritual process, to develop the life of our communities to further that goal and vision of both personal deification and corporate salvation in our Lord Jesus Christ? This task requires tremendous creativity on the part of all members of our communities, informed by grace, and infused with the inspiration of the Holy Spirit.

CHAPTER 12

Missionary Spirituality

(*Divine Ascent* No. 6)

T he Orthodox Church, over the past few centuries, has produced some extraordinary missionaries. Among these are St Nikolai of Japan, whose life and work are featured in this issue; St Innocent, a mentor of St Nikolai, and himself Enlightener of the Aleuts, first bishop of America, and finally Metropolitan of Moscow; and many others who are little known outside the places they missionized. God uses people as His instruments, to preach, teach, evangelize, to build His Church. The Orthodox Church exists in Japan because of the efforts and struggles of St Nikolai. The Orthodox Church exists in America because of the labors and struggles of St Herman and the Valaam mission of 1794, St Innocent, St Tikhon and other apostolic laborers. Certainly it is by the grace of God that the Church came to exist in these cultures. But it is also only by the cooperation of individual Christians with that grace that this happens.

Orthodoxy is a missionary Church. It always has been, and it always will be. The Byzantine Church converted half of Europe to Christ. The Russian Church converted most of northern Eurasia all the way to Alaska and even into northern California. Today, there are Orthodox Christian missionaries throughout the world working to establish the Church in many cultures where it has never existed: Madagascar, central Africa, India, the far East, Indonesia, etc. These missionaries take Christ's imperative seriously, to go into all the world, and preach the Gospel to every creature, baptizing and teaching people to follow God's commandments. The work is then carried on not only by clergy but laity as well—the real workers in the field of mission.

We have a fundamental task to follow in the footsteps of these great pioneers of our faith who struggled to fulfill the Gospel and bring those around us to faith in Christ. To do this, we must have a clear idea of what the Gospel is; we need a clear understanding, both on a rational and practical level, of what it means to be an Orthodox Christian. And we particularly need clarity in our own lives so that our own personal agendas do not get in the way of the Gospel of Christ.

It takes a particular kind of spirituality to be a missionary. Not only does it take clarity of vision as to faith and the nature and content of the tradition, but a missionary must, above all else, love people. The great missionaries are men (and women, though they are less well known) of great faith and love, and strict personal discipline. They work tirelessly and single-mindedly in the ascesis of spreading the Gospel. They are, moreover, men of vision, with an overwhelming calling and divine compulsion to preach, teach, and baptize. They inspire and make disciples of people to carry on the same work, imparting to them the same vision and experience of Christ, infecting them with the same zeal and love for the work of evangelization.

Clarity of vision comes from intensely pursuing the work of inner purification, so that the grace of God can illumine one's soul. This purification is first and foremost a renunciation of all the elements of selfishness and passionate personal agendas. Purification comes through deep repentance, confession, renunciation of one's passionate attachments and actions. It means to unite our self to Christ in the depths of our being, to cooperate with him in unity of will. The effectiveness of our preaching depends on our inner relationship with God. Our words are empty if they are hypocritical and do not proceed from deep communion. It is not enough to teach outward forms. It is the content that counts. The passions and self-centeredness erect barriers to love of the neighbor. Tearing down these barriers by repentance and purification frees one to be an instrument of God's will, manifesting the love of God. This is the real formation of a missionary.

Traditionally, most missionaries who established the Church

throughout the world were monks. Monasteries would send out brothers to establish an outpost where the Church did not already exist. Then, people would begin to gather around them and receive the message of Christ. The process would then repeat itself. This was the pattern that established Orthodoxy from the Danube to the Pacific and beyond, to Alaska.

The missionary monastery incarnated the Gospel, in charity and brotherly love, as an example to people of what the Christian life was meant to be. It formed people in the Christian life by ascetic purification, liturgical immersion and study of the Scriptures and Holy Fathers. The monks learned theology not simply by study but by practice. They learned personal discipline through monastic spiritual discipline, and applied it to the tasks at hand. As with all authentic asceticism, their discipline is based on self-denial out of love for God and neighbor. Those called by God to the ascesis of missionary activity are thus prepared by self-denial to offer themselves to Christ in love and self-sacrifice, in order to convey the Gospel. One of the greatest missionaries of the last quarter of the twentieth century, Archbishop Anastasios (Yannoulatos) of Albania, wrote:

> The question of the motive of mission can be studied from several angles: love of God and men, obedience to the Great Command of the Lord (Matthew 28:19), desire for the salvation of souls, longing for God's glory. All these, surely, are serious motives . . . However, we think that the real motive of mission, for both the individual and the Church, is something deeper. It is not simply obedience, duty or altruism. It is an inner necessity. "Necessity is laid upon me," said St Paul. "Woe to me if I do not preach the gospel"(1 Corinthians 19:16). All other motives are aspects of this need, derivative motives. Mission is an inner necessity (i) for the faithful and (ii) for the Church. If they refuse it, they do not merely omit a duty, they deny themselves. ("The purpose and motive of Mission," quoted in *Again* 22.1:7).

The great missionaries, like St Nikolai of Japan and St Innocent, gave their lives for their people. Their ascetic *podvig* ("spiritual struggle") is no less than that of the great elders and recluses. Their lives were transformed by the Gospel, transfigured by the Holy Spirit. They bore the good news of Christ not only with their lips but by the witness of their lives. They were called by God and ordained for the task of apostolic labors, and their very presence manifested the Kingdom of God.

The Gospel of Jesus Christ is the good news of the Kingdom of God. It is a message of hope, of redemption, of forgiveness, and cleansing of sins. It is what gives meaning to our lives and to our struggles. It breaks down the barriers between people, giving a common vision and purpose, uniting one to another in a bond of love that transcends culture, ethnicity, language, and all other human barriers. The message of the Gospel is the very breath of the Church, inspiring and vivifying each member. We come to a living encounter with the Living God through the Gospel, through the Church, through the sacraments. It is nothing less than that living encounter with Christ that is the essence of our message of salvation. And not only the encounter, but incorporation into His very life.

Our task, as Orthodox Christians in the West, is essentially missionary. We may not personally be called to the apostolic labor of the conversion of a whole nation (or perhaps we are?), but each one of us is called to bear witness to Christ and His Kingdom with our lives and by our faith. We must ask ourselves how we are conducting that missionary task the Lord has given us, both personally and in our parishes. We need to ask ourselves if we have a clear understanding of the message of the Gospel, and how clearly we are expressing it by our words, and incarnating it in our lives.

CHAPTER 13

Orthodoxy: Mere Christianity

(*Divine Ascent* No. 5, Presentation of the Theotokos 1999)

Christianity in Our Western Culture

Our Western culture, especially in America, has come to conceive Christianity as the most simple fundamentalism, without ritual, without sacred art, with very little intellectual or spiritual content. It is no wonder that the great bulk of well-educated young people have rejected it. Simplistic Christianity, the reduction of Christianity to a man and his Bible, going to listen to a sermon and sing some hymns on Sunday morning, and to being "nice," is simply not satisfying. The more elaborate forms, both doctrinally and liturgically, of Western Christianity, high church Protestantism and Roman Catholicism, are being equally infected with this reductionism: Under the overwhelming tide of post-enlightenment individualism, they have accepted compromises in both the moral and theological realms.

Essential Christian, Scriptural morality has been cast out, while hedonism, greed, and the gratification of the passions have become the basic values of our culture. The most essential Christian doctrines of the Resurrection of Christ, the Incarnation and the very divinity of Christ are not only questioned, but are even excised from the confessions of some "Protestant" groups. The very substance of what is left of a sacramental consciousness is being lost. While external forms may remain arguably somewhat intact, the inner spiritual and intellectual vision bears little resemblance to the apostolic faith given once and for all to the Church, and which has been taught everywhere by all at all times. We are often left with nostalgically and aesthetically pleasing cultural forms, with little or no spiritual content.

The Orthodox Sellout to the World

The Orthodox Church has fared little better in Western culture. It has condemned itself to cultural isolation by maintaining phyletist ethnic isolation from not only other Orthodox communities but from the mainline American culture itself (and thereby compromising not only its Orthodoxy but its Catholicity as well—though we are not allowed to admit that!). Perhaps this very isolation has protected it to some degree from this mortal combat with Western culture. That time is over.

Materialism threatened to destroy the Orthodox Church in its ancestral homelands, under the form of Communism. Now materialist individualism in the West undermines the essential conceptual framework of Orthodox Christians, in the relentless onslaught of consumerism and its corrupting values propagated through the media. Orthodoxy is so often reduced to a caricature: a person and "our faith" (regardless of content), some nostalgic cultural rituals on Sundays, fulfilled by their social function of bringing the community together. It is neatly compartmentalized, and has little or no impact on the rest of life, or even on one's basic belief system.

The basic values of many Orthodox Americans are those of typical American society, not of Orthodox Christianity: wealth, power, money, influence, owning the latest, the best, the most expensive home, clothes, car, computer or whatever. Family and community are subordinated to these goals, and, should they get in the way, they are dispensable. We must ask ourselves: Is the divorce rate significantly lower in the Orthodox community than elsewhere? The abortion rate?

The Loss of the Orthodox Mind

This is, of course, nothing but the "world," in Scriptural terms, and it is no different than it has ever been. What is different, though, is the degree to which it has undermined the essential Christian ethos—the Orthodox *phronema*—and placed the Orthodox Church in North America in the same position as, say, the Episcopal or Methodist Church, though with a more baroque ritual system and far quainter cultural customs. Values essential to the Orthodox faith, such as hierarchy, asceticism, self-denial and the integrity of church and family structure, have been thrown out (they are certainly politically incorrect!) and replaced with individualist egalitarianism, hedonism, and "democracy."

Even the Mother Churches of the Old World have capitulated to the demands of their sub-pubescent daughter churches and archdioceses, who insist on getting their own way. From liturgical matters, moral questions regarding the use of *economia* in clergy discipline, to the ability of the wealthy to oust an enthroned archbishop, we have a sellout of Orthodox Christianity to the world. (Of course, we must remember how many times even Constantinople sold itself out to the Papacy and became uniate, for the sake of a crusade that never came to save it from the Turks: Lyons in 1274, Florence in 1438 . . .).

Converts, and other zealots for Orthodoxy, are not immune from this temptation. While the sellout to the world may be a temptation "from the left," so the capitulation to vainglorious self-satisfaction and sectarianism is a sellout "to the right." How easily we can become obsessed with the preservation of external forms, in all their glorious traditional integrity, as a kind of guarantee of our Orthodoxy. We argue about liturgical rubrics, language, chant, iconographic style or some "issue" of calendar, ecumenism or adherence to one or another model of "canonical" ecclesiastical unity in America.

All this is vain, having the form of religion but denying its power, having an appearance of piety. Rather it is simply a justification for vainglorious hypocritical judgmentalism. How easy it is to become preoccupied with external "religious" issues, instead of confronting God in our hearts, and permitting Him to confront us. Most of these issues are simply distractions from authentic spiritual life, destructive to the unity of the One, Holy, Catholic, and Apostolic Church. There may indeed be legitimate questions, but they must be subordinated to the one thing needful, the pursuit of our common salvation in communion with one another in the One Church.

The constant preoccupation with external issues is no less a sellout to the world than ecumenism, the calendar, or liturgical renovationism. These not only distract us from the one thing needful, the salvation of our souls, but they compromise the integrity of the Orthodox Faith in its very essence, by making membership in the Church contingent on membership in the right faction. This is simply protestantism, regardless of what the rituals look like. The Orthodox Church is transformed into an exotic, esoteric sectarianism, constituted not by embracing the Catholic Faith through holy illumination and the mysteries, but by loyalty to an exclusive club, one's jurisdiction.

The Gospel gets lost in the endless polemics, and we treat each other in a shameful manner that makes a mockery of Jesus Christ and Christianity. We pride ourselves in doctrinal, liturgical, and moral integrity, but do we really believe it? If we did, there would not be such divisions among us, and we would not judge and condemn one another.

The Primacy of the Gospel in our Lives

The Gospel of Jesus Christ must be primary in the Orthodox pursuit of spiritual life. We must constantly ask ourselves if we truly believe the Gospel, if we truly believe in Jesus Christ and the salvation to which He has called us, communion through Him with the Father in the Holy Spirit. Is our faith manifest in our actions? Do we follow the commandments of the Lord to deny ourselves and take up the cross, to seek first the Kingdom of God above all things? Do we live as Christians and treat one another as Christians?

The essence of the Orthodox Christian Faith is that Jesus Christ is the incarnate Son of God, who was crucified and rose from the dead.

It is precisely this Faith that is under attack and denied by the world. It presents an ultimate challenge to the world. Not only is the Faith rationally incomprehensible; but the consequences of confessing that Faith for one's daily life are staggering. We can no longer go on living in the same way if we affirm that truth. So, it is much easier to pay it lip service, preferably in a language we don't understand, and affirm our Orthodox identity as part of our greater cultural heritage. We may do this, but if that is as far as it goes, we will go to hell.

As Orthodox Christians, we must affirm, with the Holy Fathers and the Holy Scriptures, that without this confession of Jesus Christ as Son of God there is no Christianity. That confession must not only be with our mouth, but with the entirety of our life in every aspect of every relationship. And we must affirm, with the holy martyrs and monks and saints, that that confession costs us everything, and that we can no longer live in the same way as before. Our confession of Jesus Christ as Son of God is not only with our mind, but must be lived out by our actions. We may not personally be called to die as a martyr, leave all our possessions for the sake of Christ, or become a eunuch for the sake of the Kingdom of God; only of those who can receive such a word is it required. But each and every one is commanded by Christ to deny himself, to take up his cross daily, and to follow Jesus regardless of the cost. What is required is a denial of our own will, our selfishness, our passions, and a voluntary self-offering in complete surrender to Christ.

Concrete Implications for Us

Concretely, this means that we must not surrender ourselves to the world and its values: materialism, consumerism, the desire for wealth and power. More important still, we must deny ourselves the temptation to judge and condemn one another, much less rend the seamless garment of Christ by factionalism and disputes. It means to submit ourselves as an act of self-denial in obedience to our superiors in Christ, as hard as this may be.

Only within this ascetic worldview does the life and structure of the Church, and the very confession of Jesus Christ as the Incarnate Son of God, make any sense, because it is how He lived. "He did not consider equality with God a thing to be grasped, but emptied himself, taking on the form of a servant." We must deny the world and its values: the constant gratification of our passions, and especially our pride, vainglory and self-righteousness. This is the ascetic task of every Christian, married or monastic, because it is the Way of Jesus, the Orthodox way.

Orthodoxy is mere Christianity: simple, evangelical, whole, beautiful, integral; with all the riches of grace, and centuries of saints. There is nothing superfluous, nothing left out. If we are truly Orthodox, then it will be a whole way of life, shaped by the Gospel, filled with grace, and manifest concretely in human relationships; in a communion of love, unity of mind and heart, patience, understanding and bearing one another's burdens, and charity towards our neighbors. If we fall short of this, we must blame no one but ourselves, and repent.

It is this constant repentance, turning back to Christ, denying ourselves, and crucifying ourselves to the world and its values, by which we live as Orthodox Christians. It makes Orthodoxy not only the form of religion, but the power of God to transform the world, one soul at a time.

CHAPTER 14

The Cross of Catholicity

(*Divine Ascent* No. 3–4, Entry of the Theotokos 1998)

Whether we like it or not, we have an American Orthodox Church. The current controversies in various jurisdictions have helped many Orthodox Christians realize that they are first and foremost American Orthodox Christians living and working in North America. Even those with strong ethnic identities have recognized that they are not living in diaspora but are part of a uniquely American Orthodox Church experience. A unique American Orthodox identity has evolved and is evolving, not only among converts but among "cradle Orthodox" as well, people of all jurisdictions on this continent.

This identity, however, is not reflected in the life, much less the organization, of our Church in North America. Because of this discontinuity between the identity of the Church and her organization, the Church's very life, her Orthodoxy and her Catholicity, are imperiled.

It is imperative that we establish a united Church, a single hierarchy, a ruling synod and primate, for all the Orthodox in this continent, a synod fully responsible and accountable for the entire Orthodox community in North America.

We must dismantle the multiple overlapping jurisdictions. Not only does the existence of multiple jurisdictions support competing parallel hierarchical structures and ministries. It also fosters distinct identities that exclude Orthodox Christians of other ethnic origins. It attempts to preserve ethnic national identities in a vain battle against the very culture that their people embraced when they came to America. Jurisdictional pluralism elevates ethnic identity and ecclesio-political affiliation to a level beyond the fundamental identity of Orthodox Christian. Jurisdictional pluralism does more than impede the mission of Orthodoxy in this country: It destroys it. Must one convert to an ethno-political agenda in order to unite with Christ? Such are the results of the heresy of phyletism.

At stake are fundamental ecclesiological principles, for the existence of multiple jurisdictions is not only uncanonical, it is clearly heretical. Not only does it violate the Apostolic canons, but even more essentially, it violates the Church's very Catholicity. The Orthodox Church, if she is truly the One, Holy, Catholic, and Apostolic Church, must be for all people, all Orthodox Christians, regardless of cultural identity. Catholicity must not only be vertical, maintaining the historical integrity of the fullness of the apostolic teaching and identity handed on from age to age. It must be horizontal as well, embracing all people who share that fundamental identity. We cannot juxtapose an Eastern definition of "fullness" with a Western definition of "universality." Rather, if we are Orthodox we must see Catholicity as both fullness and universality. Where there is no Catholicity, there is no Orthodoxy.

The essence of the Orthodox form of ecclesiastical organization and structure, which maintains both Orthodoxy and Catholicity, is the ascending structure of territorial communities: parishes and ministries, dioceses, archdioceses, patriarchates. The Catholicity of the Church is realized by all the Orthodox Christians in a particular area united in a single structure of conciliarity, no matter what the human particulars of ethnicity, language, or social class are. Those structures are personified—recapitulated—in the bishop and the synod with its presiding hierarch. The territorial basis for the Church's organization, in which there can be no overlapping jurisdictions, is essential for maintaining the Catholicity of the Church not just in terms of her universality, but in terms of her very Orthodoxy, her unity of mind and vision, by her common life. Concretely, it is a system of accountability and discipline, embodied in the Canons. *Sobornost*, meaning both the fullness and the universality, is the Church's very identity, throughout time and space. It is the "unity of the Spirit in the bond of peace" (Ephesians 4:3).

The conciliar functioning of the Church maintains its Catholicity by shared mutual responsibility for the integrity of the faith and discipline. It is not a function of the hierarchy alone, but of the whole community of the faithful. The bishop personifies—recapitulates—the local church in himself and is the focal point of that unity. While a local diocese may be the fullness of the Church sacramentally, it must be in communion with the other Orthodox Churches, both with other dioceses and with the Church as a whole worldwide. The various levels of synods hold the bishops accountable to one another for their stewardship of the Church's life and faith, precisely by maintaining or excluding from communion. Thus, there can be no Catholicity without Orthodoxy.

There needs to be a ministry of unity—the "Petrine" ministry—within the Church. That is precisely the position of a bishop in his diocese or the primate of a national Church, be he pope, patriarch, metropolitan, or archbishop. The primate's authority proceeds from the other bishops who elect him and with whom he has mutual accountability. This mutual accountability only works when it is incarnated on the local level, among all the bishops of a given area, to ensure the local Church's Catholicity. The integrity of the Church, her Orthodoxy and her Catholicity, proceed from the bottom up, not the top down, in this system of conciliarity and shared responsibility for the Faith. There is no sacramental mystery of ordination beyond that of bishop, and no bishop has any jurisdiction in the diocese of another. Thus, there can be no "super-episcopacy" in the Orthodox Catholic Church. There can be no such thing as universal jurisdiction. Primacy is functional, not sacramental. These are fundamental principles of the Holy Canons, of Orthodox ecclesiology, which proceed from this type of conciliar system or organization.

However, in our contemporary situation in America, with its array of "canonical" jurisdictions, each subordinate to a different patriarch, the basic principles of our ecclesiology are violated. Suddenly, beginning in the 1920s, all the patriarchs acquired universal, non-territorial jurisdiction. Yet this is precisely the problem the Orthodox have with Rome! No jurisdiction in America is accountable to any other. Instead, there is only accountability to a patriarch or synod ten thousand miles away—and often dependant on its American archdiocese for its support or survival. Thus, there is virtually no accountability and no conciliarity. And without these, there is no Catholicity. It is only by a thread that Orthodoxy itself is maintained.

We are accountable to one another as Orthodox Christians for the integrity of the faith. We cannot rely on distant foreign hierarchies for the validation or integrity of our faith or the life of our local churches. We must be united with them in full communion and offer support where needed. But responsibility for the integrity and fullness of the faith rests in the body of the faithful—the bishops and people together—not in some kind of papacy.

If the local churches are not Orthodox, then no external affiliation will make them so. Our jurisdictions are manifestations of ethnic communities, rather than reflections of the diversity that exists even in the Orthodox community, much less in our entire society. We have even let our churches be divided by secular politics and socioeconomic factors. This is contrary to the Orthodox Faith; it is contrary to the Catholicity of the Church. The division of Orthodoxy in America into ethnic jurisdictions is nothing other than phyletism. This defined heresy is an abrogation of the Catholicity of the Church by ethnic exclusiveness and chauvinism. It is not solely a matter of ethnicity, however. It is also characteristically American: that Protestant sectarianism that has created twenty-five thousand denominations, according to taste in theology, worship, race, caste, and socioeconomic status.

We labor under a false assumption that by preserving the ethnic purity of a particular archdiocese, both in terms of expression and leadership, we preserve the integrity of the Tradition. Rather, we sacrifice Orthodoxy by destroying its Catholicity. The hierarchical organization of the Church must reflect and foster the unity of the Orthodox identity of the faithful, regardless of ethnic tradition. The multiplicity of traditions, liturgical, musical, linguistic, and folk, have their place not on the level of hierarchical organization, but in the lives of the various communities. Otherwise, we are on the road to ethnic-based sectarianism.

There is no need to transform the lives of our communities into a homogeneous, all-English, "American Orthodoxy." It is an organic process of evolution and cannot be forced; but it can, and must, be encouraged. There is no need to make all Orthodox in North America conform to a single, uniform practice. Nor is it necessary to homogenize each particular community's practice and expression—whether that of a single parish or of an entire archdiocese—to some distinct ethnic model. After all, cultural pluralism or multiculturalism is at the core of the American reality. The Orthodox Tradition balances unity and diversity: unity in the Holy Mysteries manifested by unity of the hierarchy, concretely expressed in a single local synod of bishops; and diversity of expressions manifested in parishes, ethnic ministries, and organizations.

We must not only unite the upper levels of administration, we must also be faithful to the basic Orthodox ecclesiological principle of one bishop for each city, with no overlapping jurisdiction. This "territorial imperative" is at the core of our ecclesiology.

Unity and cooperation is the fruit of the maturity of the mission of the Church in this country. It proceeds from a realization that we must assume responsibility for ourselves, our church, and our faith if indeed we are to be Orthodox Christians. These are questions not only of maturity, but identity as The Church. We are no longer immigrants in diaspora, or an exile church: We are not awaiting the day of return to our homeland. North America is our homeland, and this culture is the context of our identity. Our true identity is only found in the Kingdom of God, not in any distant "old country." Thus, our Church in this country must no longer be divided by worldly identities that prevent us from living according to our true identity in Christ. Formerly, those ethnic and social identities aided us in preserving the integrity of Orthodoxy in this culture. Now we have realized that they can be a hindrance to the Church's mission and a source of division. We are united by our common Orthodox Faith and our American culture. If we are truly Orthodox Christians, our unity in the Faith is far stronger than our divisions according to ethnic origin. Our common culture has given us a context in which to work together, where we may embrace our diversity by overcoming its divisiveness. Now is the time to come together as a single Orthodox Church in North America, not by creating another "ethnic," "American" jurisdiction, but a single canonical national Church embracing all the Orthodox in this country. This is the fulfillment of the work begun by all the Old World patriarchates when they established missions in this country. We must seek their blessing to fulfill the calling God has given us, that their work might bear its rightful fruit, lest their branches be ultimately found barren.

Let us take up the cross of Catholicity, the challenge to be truly the One Holy Catholic Church in America: truly Orthodox in faith and worship and truly Catholic, incarnating the fullness in a unity of the mind, the heart, and the life of all who share the identity of Orthodox Christian. This is not a matter of church politics. It is a matter of our salvation, our stewardship of the gift of the Holy Spirit given and received in Baptism, Chrismation, and Ordination. It is our responsibility before God. Or else, how will we possibly answer the Lord Jesus Christ on the fearsome Day of Judgement for our stewardship of His Church, His Body, His mission, His presence in the world?

CHAPTER 15

Episcopacy, Primacy, and the Mother Churches

A MONASTIC PERSPECTIVE

(A Paper delivered at the Conference of the Fellowship of St Alban
and St Sergius, St Vladimir's Seminary, June 4–8, 2008)

A prominent Orthodox theologian has remarked that he thinks bishops have become useless. And he is only echoing a widespread and long-standing sentiment in our tradition. This is clear evidence of a crisis of episcopal leadership and primacy in the Church, a crisis that cuts to the heart of the apostolic and catholic identity of the Church.

While most of the problems I will address in this paper are specific to the extraordinary situation of Orthodoxy in America, they have broader application because they reveal the crisis of primacy on the ecumenical level. (And I use "ecumenical" to refer to the *oikumene*—the whole Orthodox Catholic Church). They also reveal the challenge to the Church's organization and ecclesiology posed by the new political and cultural realities of the third millennium.

Vision and Mission

The nature of Church leadership stems directly from the nature of the Church's vision. The only true vision of the Orthodox Catholic

Church is the Kingdom of God revealed in Jesus Christ, in other words, the Gospel. And all levels of Church leadership have the task of constantly renewing this vision. The Liturgy is the core of this constant renewal. It provides for us the icon of the Kingdom and of spiritual ascent into Christ, raising us up into the Body of Christ and fulfilling us as the community of the Faithful.

Leadership in the Church has a single task: Constantly to call us to this repentance in order that we may be purified of all distractions which hold us back from the living vision of the Kingdom and from fulfilling the mission to make disciples who will share the same vision. It is a call to faith: To enter into the living Body of Christ which is animated by the Holy Spirit, and to receive the "mind of Christ," the shared faith of all the saints from the very beginning. This call to repentance, to membership in the Church, and hence to a share in the vision and mission of the Kingdom of God, is unequivocally addressed to all people, without any qualification by any human distinction: race, ethnicity, citizenship, or language. There is "One Lord, One Faith, One Baptism" (Ephesians 4:5), and hence, One Church. There cannot be different churches for different kinds of people.

With that shared vision and mission comes shared responsibility. Our task within the Church is also to call one another, including our leaders, to repentance. This mutual responsibility for the integrity of the Tradition and for one another is the core of conciliarity—*sobornost*: mutual accountability of the leaders to the faithful and of the faithful to the leaders. But it is the particular role of the bishops to foster this conciliarity. Conciliarity is a healthy interdependence and synergy, in which mutual responsibility and accountability function in a spirit of love and respect. This holds on all levels of ecclesial organization.

Leadership: Responsibility, Authority, and Accountability

"Remember those who rule over you, who have spoken the word of God to you, whose faith follow, considering the outcome of their conduct. Obey those who rule over you, and be submissive, for they watch out for your souls, as those who must give account" (Hebrews 13:7). At the heart of leadership within the church is the care of souls, making the leader accountable for the lives and faith of those with whom he has been entrusted. The greater the role of leadership, the greater the accountability for the model one provides by one's own life, for the integrity of one's own faith and conduct, and for one's oversight of others. This responsibility is essential to authority. Authority has two meanings, both referring to the source of the vision and mission of the Church. It consists in the constant renewal of the vision itself, its "authorship;" and the "one who authorizes" or gives responsibility to others to fulfill the mission, holding them accountable for it.

How do the elements of responsibility, authority, and accountability manifest themselves in an Orthodox theology of leadership?

The Local Church

Let us consider some basic ecclesiological principles of the Orthodox Catholic Church. There are two facets of leadership in Orthodox ecclesiology: mysteriological and organizational.

Mysteriological or sacramental leadership is vested in the bishop, giving him the responsibility to authorize and empower others, through his blessing or ordination, to participate in that ministry for the building up of the Church.

The bishop sacramentally recapitulates his community in himself by virtue of his ordination. He bears all the fullness of the grace of the priesthood. Thus, the bishop is the "hierarch," "source of sanctification" as well as "archiereus," high priest (citing the pun of St Dionysios the Pseudo-Areopagite).

The focus of the life of the Church is local: A bishop surrounded by his clergy and people, celebrating the Eucharist, is the icon of the Kingdom in all its fullness. It is the actualization of the Church as the Body of Christ. The local church headed by its bishop is itself the fullness of the Church; but the communion of these churches with each other through synods of bishops conveys the catholic identity to each level of organization. These synods, national and ecumenical, also constitute Eucharistic communities. Each is a communion of persons with a single presidency, which manifests the unity of the body of Christ.

The primates of the national churches are not "super-bishops." There is no sacramental status above the ministry of bishop, so that, according to the Church's sacramental life, all bishops are equal. Thus it is a misnomer to refer to a national church or regional synod as a "local church."

Each level of institutional organization expresses the Church and its catholicity in a particular place. The essential principle of organization, and hence jurisdiction, is that it is geographically and politically defined. This principle is expressed by one bishop in each city, and one Synod in each region, with the president of that synod as the primate. This held true for the Roman Papacy as well as all other local and regional churches.

Catholicity

The catholicity of the Church has two dimensions: the integrity of its orthodoxy and the universality of its mission. The local Church is the fundamental principle of Orthodox ecclesiology because it bears the fullness of sacramental life, the fullness of Apostolic faith and practice. Though there may be multiple ministries for diverse needs within the population—language, culture, or other demographic issues—all the Christians in each diocese are the responsibility of that one bishop. Thus the local church is truly Catholic, embracing all elements of human diversity within itself. Its catholicity, however, depends also on its communion with other churches in the common faith and practice. Neither sense of catholicity is possible without the bishop.

This is so because the local bishop bears responsibility both for the internal integrity of his church as well as for its relationship with the other churches. It is through its bishop's presence on the synod that the local church relates to other local churches. The bishop is the point of accountability for that unity, both to his flock and to the synod in relation to them.

In the apostolic vision, the essence of primacy is episcopal leadership. Every bishop occupies the chair of Peter that preserves the unity and integrity of Peter's Faith. There is only one episcopate, which each bishop possesses equally and completely.

A "national church" is actually the synod of bishops, which elects a president from among its members. Their unity is a sign of the unity of the whole Body, and it is expressed in the person of the primate, who, as the agent of accountability, is responsible for fostering unity and communion. The primate, in turn, relates this synod and its local churches to the other national churches by maintaining doctrinal and sacramental communion with them.

There can be no primacy without synodality, and no synodality without primacy. The primate is one among the others, first among equals; yet is given the responsibility of holding the others to accountability. The authority of the primate arises from the mutual consent of those who elect him, and his acceptance by the greater community of primates throughout the world. Real primacy is an active role of actual leadership, of responsibility and accountability, in the context of actual jurisdiction.

Issues Regarding Primacy in the Orthodox Church

> The bishops of every nation must acknowledge him who is first among them and account him as their head, and do nothing of consequence without his consent. But each may do those things only which concern his own parish and the country places which belong to it. But neither let him, who is the first, do anything without the consent of all, for so there will be unanimity, and God will be glorified through the Lord in the Holy Spirit. —Apostolic Canon 34

Autocephaly and Primacy

Is there a primacy beyond that of the national church, and, if so, what is its role? The principle of the autocephaly of national synods has become the quintessential ecclesiological stance of the Orthodox Churches. According to this principle, each national synod has complete independence in governing its own affairs, and especially in electing its bishops and primate. The double office of a primate is to foster communion between the bishops and local communities through the regional and ecumenical synods, as well as to maintain relationships with other national churches.

There has been no active "ecumenical synod" that embraces all Orthodox; and there has been no ecumenical council for over 1200 years. The idea of the Ecumenical Patriarchate is based on primacy over an empire-wide synod, or ecumenical council. Indeed, canonically, the primacy of both Rome and Constantinople had one foundation: they were the imperial capitals. While this was feasible in the days of the Roman Empire, and later during the Ottoman Millet, it has long since changed. The Empire effectively ceased to exist eight hundred years ago, and now only the Greek ethnic churches, and a few others, recognize the Ecumenical Patriarchate as their real leader.

Autocephaly without an overarching primacy has given rise in the national churches to an exaggerated self-sufficiency and to the blending of national or ethnic identity with that of Orthodox Christianity. Cultural and political agendas have become central to the missions of these churches. For many believers these agendas are intermingled with or even supersede the Gospel. Ethnos and culture—not Christ— have come to determine identity.

As a result, worldwide there are few expressions of a unified Orthodox Church beyond those of Eucharistic concelebration and a few commonly enunciated positions. Even the Ecumenical Patriarchate is primarily a Greek ethnic institution, unabashedly promoting Hellenism. Ecclesiastically, this has come to mean that an Orthodox Christian's loyalty is to his ethnic homeland and to his "mother church," and that those churches maintain responsibility for all the people of their culture and nation, wherever they may be in the world.

Mother Churches and the "Diaspora"

The result is that almost all national churches have extended their jurisdictions beyond their geographic and political boundaries to the so-called diaspora. But Orthodox Christians who are faithful to the Gospel and the Fathers cannot admit of any such thing as a diaspora of Christians. Only ethnic groups can be dispersed among other ethnic groups. Yet the essential principle of geographic canonical boundaries of episcopal and synodal jurisdiction has been abrogated, and every patriarchate, every mother church, now effectively claims universal jurisdiction to serve "its" people in "diaspora." Given this fact, on what basis do we object to the Roman Papacy?

This situation arose in reaction to the mass emigration of Orthodox from their home countries, and is continued as a means of serving the needs of these immigrant communities. It is perpetuated as a means of maintaining ethnic, cultural and political identity for those away from their home country; but also as a means of financial support for the mother churches from their children abroad.

The confusion of ethnic identity and Orthodox Christian identity, expressed by competing ecclesiastical jurisdictions, is the incarnation of phyletism. Due to this confusion of the Gospel with ethnic or political identities, multiple parallel communities, each with its own allegiance to a foreign mother church, divide the Orthodox Church in North America and elsewhere into ethnic and political denominations. This distorts the Apostolic vision, and has severely compromised the catholicity of the Orthodox Churches, in which all Christians in a given territory are called to submit to a local synod of bishops.

The problem is not so much the multiple overlapping jurisdictions, each ministering to diverse elements of the population. This could be adapted as a means of dealing with the legitimate diversity of ministries within a local or national church. The problem is that there is no common expression of unity that supersedes ethnic, linguistic and cultural divisions: There is no synod of bishops responsible for all the churches in America, and no primacy or point of accountability in the Orthodox world with the authority to correct such a situation.

In the 21st century, people emigrate and move around, and Orthodox Christians need to be ministered to in their own language and with familiar traditions at least until they are acculturated. However, these should be particular ministries of the local or national church to particular groups—i.e. ministries to immigrant communities—rather than points of division. The cultural agendas of these external missions both distort the message of the Gospel and prevent people from entering into the Orthodox Church by forcing them to relinquish their own cultural identity in favor of someone else's. This also undermines any genuine missionary activity in the new land.

In reality, people do assimilate to their new cultures, and join "native" churches. This has accounted for a massive apostasy from the Orthodox Church in the West, as people find their parents' ethnic cultures, and thus the churches that promote these cultures, to be increasingly alien. This apostasy begins with the second generation, and by the fourth generation there are few that remain practicing Orthodox Christians. They leave because they were unable to find Christ and salvation through the incomprehensibility of the now alien forms and language. No matter how successful they may appear, due to new waves of immigration, churches that superimpose a national or ethnic agenda over the Gospel will die out.

Missionary Churches

But in North America there is another, very different aspect to the ecclesiological complexity. Orthodox Christianity first came to America not as an ethnic diaspora but as a missionary outreach by the Russian Orthodox Church in 1794. While the 19th century saw great immigration of Orthodox people from different countries, nevertheless the normal canonical order embracing all Orthodox of all ethnic backgrounds was observed in America, up to the 1920s, under the supervision of the Russian Mission. There was a united Synod with a single archbishop, and several bishops with missionary outreach and ministries to the various ethnic communities. But for more than a century the overwhelming needs of the new immigrant communities did make the Church in America lose sight of its original missionary purpose.

The division of the Orthodox Mission in America began in 1922 with the collapse of Russian Imperial support of the Mission following the Bolshevik coup, and the formation of parallel hierarchies, beginning with the Greek Archdiocese under Constantinople. They justified their action by a novel and idiosyncratic interpretation of Canon 28 of Chalcedon, relegating to Constantinople jurisdiction in all "barbarian lands." This was followed by the formation of several other ethnic jurisdictions, each subject to an Old World mother church. Further complications ensued as many of these communities were then divided into two or three competing segments corresponding to their various attitudes towards the political situation in their homelands, especially vis-à-vis Communism. Thus not only ethnic but political criteria distorted the message and mission of Orthodoxy in America.

However, missionary work and conversions within the Russian Metropolia and throughout the Church, continued. By the 1970s the missionary expansion of the Orthodox Church had embraced large numbers of converts, as well as the children of immigrants who had only vague identification with their ethnic roots. Today, a great majority of the clergy and laity, including the bishops, are converts or children of converts. We have an American cultural identity and a multitude of divergent ethnic and racial roots, but our primary identity is as Orthodox Christians who live in America. This missionary expansion has taken hold in all the Orthodox jurisdictions in America, even the ones that assert cultural agendas. In no way are we in diaspora.

In 1970, the Russian Orthodox Church granted autocephaly to its American mission, forming the Orthodox Church in America. While this action remains controversial to this day, it recognized the existence of a local Church in America, with the fullness of sacramental integrity and institutional self-sufficiency. In other words, the gift of autocephaly established a hierarchy with the authority to incarnate the vision and mission of the Orthodox Church in North America by its own work, and to take responsibility for the life and growth of the Church in North America while remaining accountable to the other national Churches throughout the world. Finally, there was an effort to establish church life according to canonical norms.

Some Possible Resolutions

Ecumenical Primacy

The absence of a functional ecumenical primacy within the Orthodox Church has severe implications. There is no ministry or point of unity or accountability functioning beyond the level of a national church, nothing to point to a Christian identity aside from national, linguistic, political, and cultural identities. This compromises the catholicity of the Orthodox Church, threatening division and competition between its various churches.

The Patriarchate of Constantinople is universally accepted as having a primacy of honor; but given its current situation, it is difficult for it to lead. Its claim of jurisdiction over the so-called "barbarian lands," or "diaspora" falls on the deaf ears of other patriarchates that have established identical institutions in the same territories, disregarding its claims to jurisdiction outside the geographic boundaries of existing churches.

The only way an ecumenical primacy could work is if there is a functional and active ecumenical synod, which meets at regular intervals and is composed of the heads of all the autocephalous Churches. Such a permanent synod, provided for by the canons as a permanent synod presided over by the ecumenical primate, would create a context for the up-building of the sense of unity of the Orthodox Churches, and for the resolution of particular issues as they arise. Its primate would be a point of accountability, responsible for preserving the unity and vision of the Orthodox Church. Now more than at any time in history is this feasible, given available means of communication and transportation. This would take the full cooperation of all the autocephalous churches, providing an opportunity for the Patriarchate of Constantinople to exercise real leadership, inviting the rest of the Church to unity.

Mother Churches and the "Diaspora"

The fullness of the Church is present sacramentally in a local bishop and his community; but a local church's integrity is actually compromised when its bishop belongs not to a local synod but to one in a foreign country, a synod which can neither hold its bishop accountable nor be responsible for the life of the remote diocese. We have seen this over and over again in America. The territorial structure of the Orthodox Church is rooted in very practical issues: Only through a local structure of accountability is a church able to maintain responsibility for its integrity. Outside that territorial structure, it is a disaster waiting to happen.

Being tied to a "mother church" is not of itself a guarantee of legitimacy, nor even the identity of practices and customs with those of the mother church. The canonical tradition emphasizes the integrity of the local church and its communion with the mother churches; then both its legitimacy and its tradition remain intact. The diversity of traditions within Orthodoxy is completely appropriate, but the identity of the local church has to embrace all these traditions, and respect their integrity. The common vision of the Gospel, to which all these traditions bear witness, is the underlying point of unity, and the real source of identity. We cannot make the traditions something absolute: God is the only absolute. Each tradition is unique and valuable, but is also subject to growth and change if it is alive. Ministry to people who are formed in each tradition is a legitimate function of the local church; but it is also necessary to bring all the diverse ministries and expressions, the whole People of God, into unity and coordinated action, to conciliarity. In this consists the catholicity of the Church and the role of the local bishop.

A feasible option which would both preserve the unity of the local church and minister to people of varying ethnicities and cultures would be for the "mother churches" to send clergy, even bishops, to care for the particular needs of those immigrant flocks, but who would sit on the synod of the local national church, and have their ministries coordinated through the local church. Such a bishop responsible for his ethnic missionary diocese could then be the representative of the American Church to his mother church. This could only promote a sense of unity both among the Churches and within the country, and preserve whatever flow of resources is necessary. Yet the overall vision and mission would remain the same, and the Apostolic canonical order would remain intact.

The Episcopacy: A Monastic Perspective

The role and nature of episcopal leadership within the Church is the core issue underlying all these institutional problems. All levels of episcopal primacy have been secularized, cast in terms of civil offices. Thus the patriarch is made analogous to an emperor, a bishop to a prince of the Church, etc. They even dress up in Church like Byzantine civil officials. The real nature of ministry, of arch-pastorship, and of Christian leadership, is lost.

What is the structure of leadership within the Church? On all levels, it is a structure of obedience. The presbyters are in a relationship of obedience to their bishop. The bishops are in a relationship of obedience to their primate. The primate is in the relationship of spiritual father to his bishops. Jurisdiction is about a relationship of obedience, which is precisely responsibility and accountability.

The crisis in the episcopacy is rooted in the breakdown of the basic structure of spiritual obedience, which is the essence of Orthodox Christianity. Spiritual obedience is not subjection and compliance. Rather, it is a hierarchy of love and shared responsibility, a hierarchy of discipleship. What is this but a structure of accountability in a spirit of trust and cooperation, in mutual love and respect? Moreover, it is a complex of very personal relationships. When these relationships become simply institutional, and the personal becomes relativized, the very nature of the Church, which in its very essence is about the actualization of authentic personhood, is distorted.

This breakdown comes from the secularization of the Church's structure by the centuries of imperial subjugation, by the corruption of authority into power, by the reduction of church leadership to an institutional model, and the reduction of membership in the Church to civic duty. The Faith itself was degraded from a personal commitment to Christ to a socio-political ideology. Nominal church membership and nominal Orthodox identity are the foundations of secularization. This kind of corruption began in the fourth century.

When the Church was subjected to the Roman, then Ottoman, and then Russian Empires, then to the status of state church, it was effectively reduced to a department of state. The bishops and administration of the Church assumed imperial roles, insignia, and rituals; and with them, the Christian vision of the leader as servant became a hypocritical parody. Of course, there have been notable exceptions.

This led to the separation of charismatic and institutional authority within the Church. What followed was the bureaucratization of church leadership: the reduction of the episcopacy to institutional administration, and the virtual elimination of its pastoral role. Charismatic authority within the church was tolerated among monastic elders, but had little other influence in the life of the Church from the late Byzantine period through the Turkokratia and the suppressions of monasticism in the Russian Empire. The fruit of this was the suppression of creativity and initiative, theologically and organizationally, for fear of being disciplined and rejected. Instead, personal ambition and competition for position became dominant within the church's institution. Charismatic leadership arising from spiritual vision, the fruit of asceticism, found little context to express itself, even being regarded as dangerous, in the state-controlled institution of the church.

The bishops came to wield power over the lives of their clergy, and instead of being chief pastors, they became distant administrators feared by their clergy. Obedience became confused with compliance and submission. Authority came to be identified with power, humility with subjection, and respect with adulation and sycophancy. Accountability was always referred "upwards:" the bishops to the patriarch and emperor or sultan; the priests to the bishops; while the people simply ignored the hierarchy. Even the monasteries, where the ancient vision of the apostolic church was most clearly maintained, were subjected to this secularization of power and office.

The corrupting fruit of secularization is fear and the lack of trust, hence isolation, autonomy, self-will and the breakdown of the real authority of the episcopacy. It destroys souls and the institution of the Church. Secularization reduces the Body of Christ to a religious organization; it is the form of religion, deprived of its power.

The original vision of the episcopacy was a model of spiritual discipleship, mirroring Christ and the apostles. Christ is the Master: not the master of slaves, but the teacher—not *despota* (!) but *didaskalos*. The apostles were his disciples, his students. Christ did not exercise power over his disciples, but his authority in their lives arose from their voluntary cooperation in love and respect. Thus, He no longer called them disciples, but friends. What made them friends is their obedience—not subjection, but synergy in love. Is this not the model we should be following?

But Jesus called them to Himself and said, "You know that the rulers of the Gentiles lord it over them, and those who are great exercise authority over them. Yet it shall not be so among you; but whoever desires to become great among you, let him be your servant. And whoever desires to be first among you, let him be your slave—just as the Son of Man did not come to be served, but to serve, and to give His life a ransom for man" (Matthew 20:25–28).

Spiritual Fatherhood

Christ exercised the role of spiritual father to his disciples. The role of the bishop, as well as that of any headship in the Orthodox Church, is spiritual fatherhood: pastor in a parish, abbot in a monastery, bishop in a diocese, primate in a synod. To be a spiritual father means to be a shepherd and teacher, to exhort, rebuke, and encourage his disciples in their faith, service to one another, and especially, love for one another. It means to take responsibility for the salvation of these particular others, which presumes a relationship of obedience. True obedience is offered freely in love; it is in absolute opposition to the corruption of power and control.

Spiritual obedience is precisely a structure of accountability. The disciples are accountable for their obedience to the father; but the spiritual father is responsible not only to develop each disciple to the fullness of his potential through that obedience, but to unify the whole body through his pastoral role—to keep the whole body in synergy. The authority of the spiritual father comes from the cooperation of his disciples. The spiritual father is thus accountable to his disciples. True obedience is thus a relationship of absolute mutuality. Thus, the ministry of spiritual fatherhood is a charism within the Church and for the sake of the Church, not over it. The bishops and presbyters are part of the People of God, not lords over them; as spiritual fathers, they can only function within this structure of mutual accountability and responsibility, upon which all Christian authority rests.

Christian authority cannot be imposed from above, but has its source in the voluntary cooperation of love, obedience, and mutual accountability. This is conciliarity, *sobornost*, in the true sense. The bishop recapitulates his local church in himself: this is the charism of ordination. Yet, the bishop has no authority without his church. Ordination only functions within the body of the faithful and is meaningless outside the context of the Church. While grace elevates the one ordained, that grace can only function within a context of the synergy and consensus of the Church—ultimately manifest in the Liturgy. But this vision was distorted by the conflation of the clerical hierarchy and the imperial office, spiritual authority and political power; and the divorce between charismatic and institutional leadership, thus secularizing the clergy.

In other words, the bishops elect the primate of their synod, the presbyters should elect their bishop, and monastics elect their abbot or abbess. Thus primacy, the authority of the spiritual father, proceeds from the consent of those who offer their obedience to him. And he is responsible to them and for them, as they are to him. Grace acts through them together and fulfills their synergy in unity of mind and heart in mutual love.

This model works on every level of church organization, and is the core of the evangelical, patristic, and canonical vision. In it there is no place for fear, power, or control but rather, a communion in love and mutual respect in voluntary cooperation.

Even presidency at the Eucharistic celebration is in function of this relationship. The pastor in his parish, abbot in his monastery, bishop in his diocese or primate in his synod, presides because of his role as spiritual father. He is not the spiritual father simply because he presides; this eliminates the personal dimension of ecclesial community leadership. He is the "good shepherd who gives his life for his sheep" (John 10:11). This is the ultimate accountability of the spiritual father.

The true spiritual father, like Christ, can never refer or take anything to himself. He always points to God the Father, "from whom every paternity is named." Any kind of ego gratification is spiritual death, but this is especially so in the case of spiritual fatherhood which demands kenotic humility, the death of the ego. The only way to achieve this is spiritual formation.

Spiritual formation has one goal: the ascent to spiritual maturity, to spiritual vision. Spiritual vision, or *theoría*, is a gift of grace bestowed only after one has prepared oneself to receive it by opening oneself to God through purification, leading to dispassion through ascetic discipline and contemplative prayer. Through the experience of illumination, one gains perspective on all the external forms and issues which constitute temptations. One must first transcend the ego, one must "crucify the old man who is corrupt through the passions of the flesh," in order to attain to a clarity of vision and the gift of discernment. As long as we are controlled by our passions, our motives and desires will be self-serving. Only through attaining dispassion can we be freed from the blindness of our self-centeredness, in order to truly love the other unconditionally, free from any selfish agendas. Then a man has the ability to be a true spiritual father: To discern in his disciples what holds them back from attaining dispassion and spiritual maturity, having the vision to see what each one needs to grow.

The episcopate, and all primacy, demand this kind of spiritual vision, the charismatic dimension, arising from ascetic self-discipline, in order for the bishops to discern the pastoral task for each person for whom they are responsible, and the clarity of mind to discern the path for the future. This kind of spiritual vision is necessary to discern the will of God, the Presence and the activity of God, in order to guide the church into active cooperation, synergy, with the Divine will, and to see and eliminate any personal agendas or passions which disrupt the communion of the Church with God and with one another.

Conclusion: Spiritual Fatherhood and Primacy

Real primacy is about leadership, and Orthodox spiritual leadership is inseparable from spiritual fatherhood, in which spiritual children offer their obedience in love to their spiritual fathers, who in turn care for their souls. This model holds true for a monastery with an abbot and his monks, a parish with a pastor and his flock, a diocese with the bishop and his presbyters, or a national church with the primate and his bishops. So it must also hold true on the ecumenical level.

The Church is not a civil society, with its programs, political and social influence, and worldly goals. It is rather a community built on faith in Jesus Christ, united in the common mission of the Gospel. The Church is composed of those who share an identity that comes from faith, and transcends all worldly and secular, ethnic, social, economic and racial divisions. It is the living incarnation of the Kingdom of God on earth. It embraces all human diversity, bringing all to unity in Christ.

Spiritual leadership within the Church, especially the episcopacy, has as its function to lead people into that Kingdom, to illumine and perfect them in the Faith, and thus to transform life in this world one soul at a time. This leadership is primarily a call to repentance, to re-focus on God, and to leave behind all the distractions of sin. This leadership is manifested in authentic spiritual guidance, which exorcises the corruption of sin and ego-centrism, and leads the Church in one-ness of mind and heart to the synergetic praise of God in the glorious Liturgy of the Kingdom.

CHAPTER 16

A Time of Crisis and Opportunity

(The following is a portion of the opening address of His Beatitude, Metropolitan Jonah to the OCA Metropolitan Council at their 2009 Spring Meeting, February 18, 2009.)

The past years have been a huge struggle and a time of cleansing and purgation, a true crisis in the sense of a time of judgment. The Orthodox Church in America has emerged from this crisis, realizing that much has to be changed and much has to be created anew in its internal structures. This is a time of immense opportunity. Not only did the inadequacies and sins of the past regimes create an impasse for the Church, and present it with horrific choices; but, these revealed the deeper structural flaws in the organization of the OCA that permitted and perhaps created the crisis to begin with. These include, but are not limited to, structures of accountability and delineation of responsibilities, which are not dealt with adequately in our current statute. This was complicated by a lack of appropriate leadership. As a result the central administrative organizations of the Church were thrown into disarray.

Most of the superficial problems have been dealt with, and a new administration is in place, new policies have been implemented to create structures of accountability, and there is new leadership. But the underlying issues of the inadequacies of our statute, and the confusion of responsibilities between the organs of our central organizations, constitute what our essential task is to address in the near future. There are also issues left over that are pressing, and we also need to address and resolve them, so that the Orthodox Church in America can move on and assume the responsibility of its mandate: to be the local indigenous autocephalous Orthodox Church in North America.

During our time of troubles, the national and international reputation of the OCA was severely compromised. Movement towards Orthodox unity in America was severely damaged, and the perception of the OCA as being a viable partner in any movement towards unity, or even a player, was compromised. Various other Churches expected our dissolution. But in the words of Mark Twain, "Rumors of my demise have been greatly exaggerated!"

Coinciding with this slide there has been a descent into deeper and deeper parochialism, and with that, congregationalism. This "hunker down" mentality really constitutes a loss in the catholic breadth of the vision of our Church.

The breadth of vision is the key to our renewal. During the crisis, the leadership of the Church, Episcopal, clerical and lay, became completely consumed with the "next issue" to arise, the next revelation of wrongdoing, the next betrayal or failure of some leader. The vision of the Church was buried in gossip and scandal, people became demoralized and disillusioned, and God and His Providence were forgotten. What is important to remember is that while these things did happen, evil as they were, it is the pastoral effect that must be addressed as well as the issues themselves. It is a tragic thing to see someone in a position of great responsibility fall; it is a worse thing to judge and condemn them, and then fall into resentment towards the institution and community which itself was the victim. It becomes a self-perpetuating vicious circle. What suffered is the Church as Church, as people lost sight of the Church as the Body of Christ, and instead became focused on individual members and their sins and failings. The bishops are not the Church. The Central Administration is not the Church; nor is the MC (Metropolitan Council), the AAC (All American Council) or any other organization.

Rather, we all constitute the Church, together, in Christ by the Spirit. We who are broken and sinful, dishonest and corrupt people. When we lose sight of our own sinfulness, and start blaming and judging others, we have lost our Christianity. If we want vengeance and retribution, we trample on Christ and the Gospel. We cut ourselves off from God and from one another in a great orgy of ego gratification. "Everyone loves a dirty little sex scandal." And scandals over money are not far behind. But does it not occur to us, as incensed as we are with self-righteous indignation, that all this is a distraction and temptation to betray Christ and betray ourselves as Christians? Temptation always presents this question: Will I act as a Christian, or not, in relation to this provocation?

If we have responsibility for the life of the Church, which we as the bishops and the Metropolitan Council as clerical and lay leaders do, we have to know about this stuff (Unfortunately!) in order to correct the problems. But if we allow ourselves to obsess about it, and especially in judgment and condemnation of others, not only have we forgotten our own sins and hypocrisy, but we will be blind to any constructive solution, any solution that is of God. Ultimately, all these problems came and were revealed as God's Providence for us. They revealed weaknesses that needed to be addressed, and an opportunity for us to address them.

We have to return to the vision of Christ, crucified and risen from the dead, present now, and coming again, that is at the very core of our life as the Church. To be an Orthodox Christian is to focus our lives on Jesus Christ, and to continue His ministry of love and reconciliation, the call to repentance and forgiveness. We are called to bear one anothers' burdens—the burden of one another—and so fulfill the Law of Christ (Gal 6:2). The Lord calls us to patience and longsuffering, always going by the way of humility and love. This vision of Christianity must be at the very heart of all our decisions and all our lives, as Christians, and especially as leaders of the Church.

Revisioning the Orthodox Church in America

We have an enormous opportunity, and responsibility, to re-vision the structure and life of the Orthodox Church in America. While the basic elements are outlined in the Tradition, especially the Canons of the Ecumenical Councils and the Fathers, there are other elements that we incorporate as 21st Century Americans. Those essential elements from the Tradition are the Holy Synod presided over by the Metropolitan, a diocesan structure, and the canonical heritage. Other values critical to us, and partly coming from the Russian Council of 1917, are the participation of lay and clerical members in decision making. The Strategic Planning process on which we are embarking is precisely the process we are using to re-vision the Church.

Ultimately, we need to rewrite the Statute. The structures that were put in place and incorporated in the Statute reflected the life of the Metropolia and its early transition to being the autocephalous Orthodox Church in America. When the Statute was written, the OCA consisted essentially of a single archdiocese, with three or four sub-dioceses, with bishops who were essentially auxiliaries. It was a fairly homogenous social and ethnic community located mainly in the "Rust Belt" between Chicago and New York, north of the Ohio River. Cultural ideas of egalitarianism, democracy and division of powers, as well as identity as a corporation, shaped the initial document. Transparency, accountability and "best practices" had not even entered the national debate.

The OCA has outgrown its previous structures. It has become a huge, diverse community stretching to every corner of the continent. It consists of 13 dioceses, each with its own life. It is largely a convert church, and has no social, ethnic or linguistic homogeneity—and is authentically local and indigenous, rather than an ethnic church. While culturally very North American (in its own diversity), the OCA can no longer be "one of the jurisdictions," but rather has to develop its internal structures to measure up to the challenge of being the Local Autocephalous Church, inclusive of the tremendous diversity of our continent, but also respecting the uniqueness of each community and its needs.

The Statue itself and the organizations it creates have become obsolete. The AAC not only has become huge and unwieldy, and cannot effectively make most decisions; but the real underlying problem is that it compromises the diocesan structure of the Church, treating the whole Church as a single archdiocese with parish representation. The MC was initially the archdiocesan council, advising the one bishop with full authority, the Metropolitan. The central administration performs all the statutory functions of the Metropolitan Council; and then we wonder why there is conflict. The crisis created a power vacuum, which the MC stepped in to fulfill—a power gap previously filled by the Chancellor. But nowhere in the Statute is the MC given any authority as an organ of accountability; BUT neither is anyone one else specifically. Nor does the MC perform the primary role defined in the Statute: as the main fiduciary, to raise the money to support the life and work of the church. Because the leadership was dysfunctional, the Holy Synod abrogated its authority, and retreated into their own dioceses; the central administration grew to immense proportions and power, and both the Holy Synod and the Metropolitan Council rubber stamped the decisions of the CA, and abrogated their responsibility. Et cetera.

"... And so, my dears, we have a mess." Not to even bring up any corruption. So where do we start? First, we have to look at basic Orthodox ecclesiology. The Apostles invested the bishops with the leadership of the Church, through sacramental ordination. This is the principle of authority in the Church: sacramental responsibility. This sacramental responsibility is not only over what is "spiritual," but the entire life of the whole Church, in every aspect, because even how we use our money is spiritual and sacramental. There can be no dualism between the spiritual and the material.

The real underlying question is the issue of leadership—primatial, Episcopal and lay. We need to examine the nature of primacy: How the episcopacy relates to the local church, and the interrelationship of the local churches within their province, and hence, the role of the Metropolitan as Primate. Central to this, however, is the nature of that relationship of obedience: of the presbyters to the bishop, and the bishops to the Metropolitan. Primacy is constituted by accountability and authority, in a relationship of obedience. This is Christian leadership. All of this is, ultimately, defined in the ancient Canons, and rooted in the Scriptures.

"Obey those who rule over you, and be submissive, for they watch out for your souls, as those who must give account. Let them do so with joy and not with grief, for that would be unprofitable for you" (Heb. 13:17).

I believe that the starting place to understand all this is to understand authority and obedience as responsibility, rather than as "power." Any reduction to "power" is by definition, corruption. Accountability in relation to responsibility is a core element in obedience. Various areas of responsibility are given to the different offices and organs of the Church by the canons. The question is, how are they invested with responsibility and for what, and to whom they are accountable? Accountability is intimately linked with responsibility; the structures of accountability are built as structures of obedience. Then we have to look at the nature of the support of the whole structure: first, financially, with the flow of money and resources; then, the flow of responsibility and accountability in relation to the organs of advice and consensus.

Bishops and the Metropolitan

The bishops of every nation must acknowledge him who is first among them and account to him as their head, and do nothing of consequence without his consent. But each may do those things only which concerns his own parish [diocese] and the country places which belong to it. But neither let him, who is the first, do anything without the consent of all, for so there will be unanimity, and God will be glorified through the Lord in the Holy Spirit (Apostolic Canon 34).

The basic unit of the Church is the diocese: the bishop surrounded by the presbyters, deacons and faithful. The bishop has responsibility for the whole body, and sacramentally recapitulates it, and all ministries flow from the bishop. This is the literal meaning of "hierarch"—the "source of all priesthood." The presbyters and deacons, in particular, as well as all the faithful, are in a relationship of obedience to the bishop, and accountable to him for their service within the Church. The bishop has a double accountability: to the clergy and laity of his diocese; but also to the Synod which elected him as its head.

The Synod of bishops of a nation is the "Local Church." They bear responsibility for the oversight of all the churches in their care. They have the responsibility to elect and install new bishops where there is a vacancy or need. They are the point of accountability for each other. They elect as president of their Synod the bishop of the metropolis or "mother city," as Metropolitan Archbishop.

The Metropolitan bears the responsibility to maintain unanimity and consensus among the bishops in all matters affecting the life of the Church as a whole, and is the point of accountability for the bishops; while he in turn is accountable to them. This is a relationship of obedience, accountability in mutual love and respect, for the responsibilities given. The Metropolitan has the responsibility to relate his Local Church to the other Local Churches, and maintain unity and communion. This "ecumenical level" is the highest level of accountability, as it is the final court of appeal. The Metropolitan is a diocesan bishop, as are all the others. Thus all the bishops of the Synod bear an equal responsibility, as well as an equal ordination. The one thing that distinguishes the ministry of the Metropolitan is his primacy: his responsibility to be the point of accountability, with the other bishops in a relationship of obedience. There is no "super-bishop" or ordination over that of bishop.

> The presiding Bishop in a metropolis must be recognized by the Bishops belonging to each province (or eparchy), and undertake the cure of the entire province, because of the fact that all who have any kind of business to attend to are wont to come from all quarters to the metropolis. Hence it has seemed best to let him have precedence in respect of honor, and to let the rest of the Bishops do nothing extraordinary without him, in accordance with the ancient Canon of the Fathers which has been prevailing, or only those things which are imposed upon the parish of each one of them and upon the territories under it. For each Bishop shall have authority over his own parish, to govern in accordance with the reverence imposed upon each, and to make provision regarding all the territory belonging to his city, as also to ordain Presbyters and Deacons, and to dispose of details with judgment, but to attempt nothing further without the concurrence of the Bishop of the

Metropolis; nor shall he himself, without the consent and approval of the rest (Regional Council of Antioch: 9).

There is a fundamental difference in primacy between a diocese and a synod. In a diocese there is a distinct difference in responsibility and structure of accountability because the levels of ordained responsibility are unequal. In a diocese, the bishop presides by virtue of his ordination, and all the clergy and people are accountable to him for their stewardship; as well as he to them for his leadership. In the Synod, it is a community of equals, all bishops, though the Metropolitan has primacy.

The Metropolitan's ministry is to hold the bishops to accountability in a structure of obedience that is by its very nature love and respect, unanimity and synergy. The Metropolitan's leadership arises through building consensus, rather than authority over the other bishops. Decisions are communal, by consensus; and the Metropolitan cannot act alone. As a bishop sacramentally recapitulates his diocese, so also the Metropolitan recapitulates the Synod, personifying it and speaking for it. The Metropolitan cannot intervene in the affairs of another diocese, unless there is a canonical issue; then that intervention is his responsibility on behalf of the Synod. A diocesan bishop is accountable to the Synod for his stewardship of the diocese, because he is given that responsibility by them in election and ordination in a relationship of obedience. That structure of accountability is personified in the relationship of obedience to the Metropolitan.

A bishop's authority comes from his responsibility for his own diocese; the metropolitan's authority is within the Synod. The parishes relate to their own bishop, as their point of accountability in obedience. The bishops relate to one another in the Synod as the structure of accountability in obedience to the Metropolitan. But, the Metropolitan, as metropolitan, has no relationship to either the parishes or the clergy directly, other than those in his own diocese. This is very important, especially in regards to the flow of resources.

The Metropolitan's responsibilities, as primate, are in maintaining unity among the bishops of his Synod, and resolving whatever decisions need to be made on a Synodal level, and whatever issues directly affect the whole Church. The primacy also demands that the Metropolitan relate his Synod to the other Local Churches, maintaining recognition, contact, and communion. This would include, in our contemporary situation, relations with other jurisdictions in America, as well as with the other Autocephalous Churches. Thus, all matters related to the transfer of clergy between Churches, jurisdictional disputes, and so forth, are within the purview of the Metropolitan. It is also within his purview to convene the Synod, councils and church-wide conferences; oversee church-wide ministries such as theological education; and oversee economic matters such as tax status, legal matters and insurance which affect the whole Church. The Metropolitan oversees matters dealing with bishops, including election, placement, accusations, investigations, transfers, and canonical actions.

Administration

> The bishop is entrusted with responsibility for every aspect of the life of the Church, including full authority over the material goods and finances of the Church. —Apostolic Canon 41

> We ordain that the bishop have authority over the goods of the Church, for if he is to be entrusted with the precious souls of men, much more are temporal possessions to be entrusted to him. He is therefore to administer them all of his own authority, and supply those who need, through the presbyters and deacons, in the fear of God, and with all reverence. He may also, if need be, take what is required for his own necessary wants, and for the brethren to whom he has to show hospitality, so that he may not be in any want. For the law of God has ordained, that they who wait at the altar should be maintained at the altar's expense. Neither does any soldier bear arms against an enemy at his own cost.

As this reflects the practice of the 4th Century and before, the later canons bring up the practice of a steward or *economos*, essentially chancellor or treasurer, to assist in the management of the affairs of the diocese. This is the beginning of diocesan administration other than through cathedral deacons and presbyters.

> Since in some churches, as we have been informed, the Bishops are administering the ecclesiastical affairs with the services of a Steward, it has seemed most reasonable and right that each and every church that has a Bishop should also have a Steward selected from its own Clergy to manage the ecclesiastical affairs of that particular church in accordance with the views and ideas of its own Bishop, so as to provide against the administration of the church being unwitnessed, so as to prevent the property of the same church from being wasted as a result of such stewardless administration and to prevent any obloquy from attaching itself to holy orders (Chalcedon: 26).

In the Orthodox Church, according to the Canons, all responsibility rests ultimately on the bishops: spiritual as well as financial and organizational. They may and should designate people to handle such affairs, both for the sake of ability to administer and to guard the reputation and integrity of the bishop. This is where we can begin to see the foundation of the central and diocesan administrations, as well as the Metropolitan Council.

Vision for Today and the Future

The OCA is the heir of this ancient tradition, and structures its life accordingly. However, over the past decades, this system broke down to some extent because of personalities involved, and to a great extent because it went out of balance. The dioceses, to a great extent, did not take on the full responsibility for their own lives, and the Metropolitan and his staff took on the role of an archdiocese—or rather, continued it according to the existing statute. In the meantime the life of the Church grew and developed, dioceses were formed that assumed responsibility over their own lives—"sovereignty."

What we need now is for the dioceses to develop fully, and each to take on responsibility for itself. Each diocese needs to develop its own programs, funding, and missionary outreach. At the same time, the Metropolitan's Office must focus on the things that are in its purview, and leave the dioceses to handle their own business. Clergy matters, internal OCA transfers, local ministries, youth programs, development of missions, charitable and evangelistic outreach are all the responsibilities of each diocese and its bishop.

The Metropolitan's Office has the responsibility to take care of the administrative tasks that affect the whole church. The Office of the Metropolitan, perhaps a better name than "central administration," is called to focus on coordinating diocesan programs for ministries, as well as the intra- and inter-Orthodox relations that are necessary, and develop programs that benefit the whole Church. This requires a staff, as prescribed by the Statute. How large a staff is a different question. Clearly the 37 people on staff, more employees than all the dioceses put together, and a bigger budget than all the dioceses put together, was excessive. How large that staff should be also depends on how much the dioceses are ready to assume their responsibilities. This is not possible until the dioceses are adequately funded.

Another element is the place of the All American Council. The All American Council, as a legislative body per the 1971 Statute, does not work. The AAC does not reflect the diocesan structure of the Church. It treats the whole OCA as a single archdiocese, with one bishop. This is simply not the reality. While the value of lay participation in decision making is almost universally accepted, the scope of the council is too large to allow for meaningful discussion, especially as it affects the life of each particular diocese. The council allows for no contact or discussion, much less constant interaction, of the bishop with the delegates from his diocese. But especially problematic is the fact that the Council treats each parish as belonging to the greater OCA, rather than its own diocese. As a result of this unwieldiness, the Metropolitan Council has taken on the legislative function of the AAC.

The Metropolitan Council is structured like a board of trustees, according to the laws of New York State, where the OCA is incorporated. There are two issues here: The administration in the Metropolitan's Office performs most of the statutory responsibilities of the MC, while others are done by both. Many of these functions, book- and record keeping and coordination, can only be done by a standing administration. The main fiduciary responsibility is in fact given to the Metropolitan Council by the Statute, both for budget as well as for raising funds and supporting the work of the whole Church. Even this was taken over by the Central Administration of old, by a Development Office. The Metropolitan Council needs to turn its attention and considerable talent to the challenge of raising financial support for the Church. There are two elements in this: a development function for donations, trusts, bequests and so forth; and a church-wide rethinking of support, based on the principles of percentage giving or tithing. More later on this.

The second structural issue, however, is more problematic. The laws for religious corporations pertain primarily to parishes, and not to the structure of a synodal Church. On the parish and diocesan levels, the rector and the bishop have full responsibility and accountability for use of resources, and the bishop in particular canonically. In a parish, the Parish Council, led by the priest, has the responsibility to manage the financial and material resources of the parish; in a diocese, the Diocesan Council, led by the bishop. As long as the presiding clergyman is the president of the Council, there is no problem: the Council has the responsibility to assist the priest or bishop in the administration of the material resources as trustees.

The Synod, however, and the Office of the Metropolitan as the organizational recapitulation of the Synod, is different. While the MC started out as an archdiocesan council, with the above function, as the Church has grown into a fully functioning Synodal structure, the structure of the MC has to change. It is the bishops who bear the primary fiduciary responsibility for the Church according to the Canons. The MC shares that responsibility, but on a different level. The Metropolitan and Synod have to approve or can veto decisions of the MC; the Metropolitan Council cannot veto decisions of the Synod.

This can be resolved in that it must be made clear in the new Statute that the bishops, collectively as the Synod, bear the main responsibility and accountability for the material resources, as well as the spiritual life, of the Church. The MC executes their decisions, and administers the resources of the Church, providing for its maintenance and ministries; but it does not have the same level of accountability as the Synod itself, nor can it make decisions independently of the Synod and/or Metropolitan—which is already clear in the existing statute.